French - English

LEARNING FLASHCARDS

FOR BABIES TODDLERS

alligator

alligator

The alligator is having a party.

fourmi

ant

The ant is red.

ours

bear

The bear loves you.

abeille

bee

The bee is saying hello.

oiseau

bird

The bird is flying.

papillon

butterfly

The butterfly is pretty.

chameau

camel

The camel has a hump.

chat

cat

The cat is happy.

dinosaure

dinosaur

The dinosaur is laying eggs.

poulet

chicken

The chicken is dancing.

vache

cow

The cow has a bell.

cerf

deer

The reindeer has a toy.

chien

dog

The dog has two floppy ears.

dauphin

dolphin

The dolphin is swimming.

canard

duck

The duck has a bow.

aigle

eagle

The eagle is looking for food.

l'éléphant

elephant

The elephant is sitting.

poisson

fish

The fish is a clownfish.

libellule

dragonfly

The dragonfly is blue.

renard

fox

The fox has a red nose.

grenouille

frog

The frog is smiling.

girafe

giraffe

The giraffe has a long neck.

chèvre

goat

The goat has a beard

ver de terre

worm

The worm is in the apple

poule

hen

The hen has chicks.

hippopotame

hippopotamus

The hippo is big.

cheval

horse

The horse is fast.

kangourou

kangaroo

The kangaroo has a baby.

chaton

kitten

The kitten is playing.

lion

lion

The lion has a mane.

homard

lobster

The lobster is red.

singe

monkey

The monkey has a tail.

poulpe

octopus

The octopus has food.

hibou

owl

The owls have big eyes.

panda

panda

The panda wears a diaper.

porc

pig

The pig is fat and pink.

chiot

puppy

The dog is brown.

lapin

rabbit

The rabbit has a carrot.

rat

mouse

The mouse is writing something.

crabe

crab

The crab has two pinchers.

requin

shark

The shark is scary.

mouton

sheep

The sheep are very fluffy.

escargot

snail

The snail is slow.

serpent

snake

The snake has poison.

araignée

spider

The spider is purple.

écureuil

squirrel

The squirrel has a nut.

tigre

tiger

The tiger has a red bow.

tortue

turtle

The turtle has a shell.

loup

wolf

The wolf is smiling.

zèbre

zebra

The zebra is black and white.

dinde

turkey

The turkey has two legs.

coq

rooster

The rooster will crow.

perroquet

parrot

The parrot is colorful.

hérisson

hedgehog

The hedgehog has apples.

pomme

apple

The apple has a leaf.

abricot

apricot

The apricot is yellow.

avocat

avocado

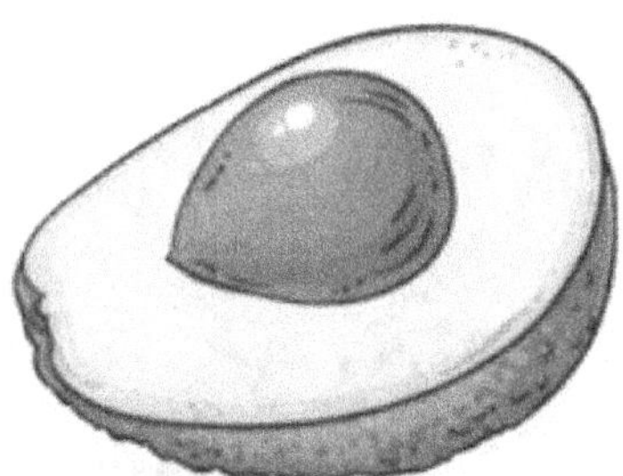

The avocado has a nut.

banane

banana

The banana is yellow.

la mûre

blackberry

There are a lot of blackberries.

cassis

blackcurrant

The blackcurrants are yummy.

myrtille

blueberry

The blueberries are sweet.

cerise

cherry

The cherries have a stem.

noix de coco

coconut

The coconuts have juice.

figues

fig

The fig has seeds.

grain de raisin

grape

The grapes are purple.

pamplemousse

grapefruit

The grapefruits are sour.

kiwi

kiwi

The kiwi is fresh.

citron

lemon

The lemons are yellow.

citron vert

lime

We have lots of lime.

litchi

lychee

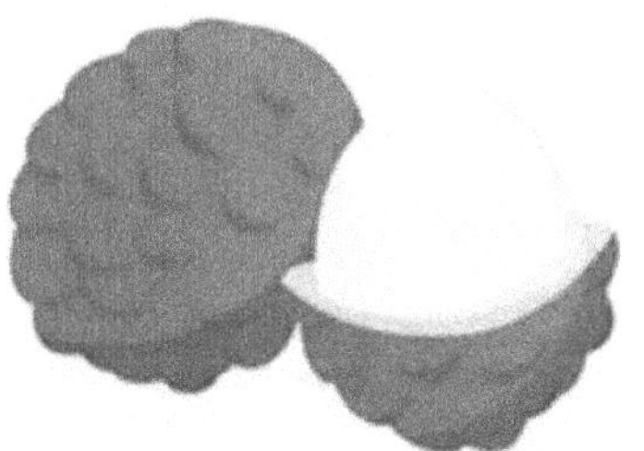

I like to eat lychee.

mandarine

mandarin

Oranges are refreshing.

mangue

mango

Mango is my favorite fruit.

orange

orange

Mandarins are like oranges.

papaye

papaya

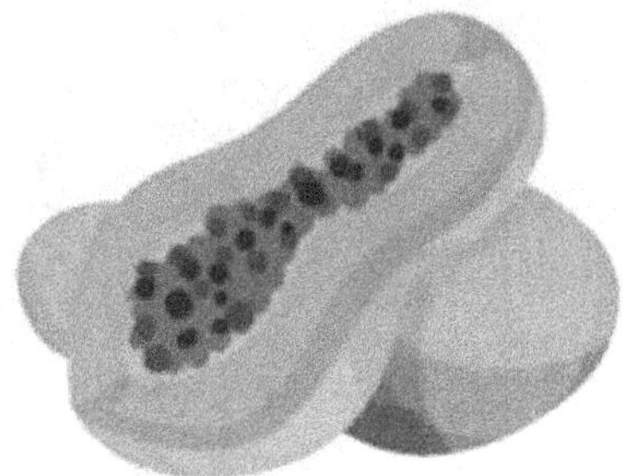

Papayas have lots of seeds.

pêche

peach

Peaches are juicy.

poire

pear

Pears have a strange figure.

ananas

pineapple

The pineapple has a thumbs up.

prune

plum

Plums are healthy for you.

grenade

pomegranate

Pomegranates are all red.

framboise

raspberry

The raspberry is shiny.

fraise

strawberry

The strawberry has leaves on top.

pastèque

watermelon

The watermelon is big.

mandarine

tangerine

The tangerine looks like an orange.

tarte

pie

I like to eat apple pie.

gâteau

cake

That cake is huge.

bonbons

candy

Candy is not good for your teeth.

biscuit

cookie

Cookies are easy to make.

donut

donut

I like strawberry donuts.

crème glacée

ice cream

The ice cream is melting.

muffin

muffin

The muffin has a cute wrapper.

pudding

pudding

We eat pudding on Christmas.

classeur

binder

I keep pictures in my binder.

livre

book

I like to eat books.

sac à dos

backpack

The backpack has lots of stuff.

les ciseaux

scissors

I have scissors in my bag.

épingles

pins

Pins can hold stuff up.

agrafe

clip

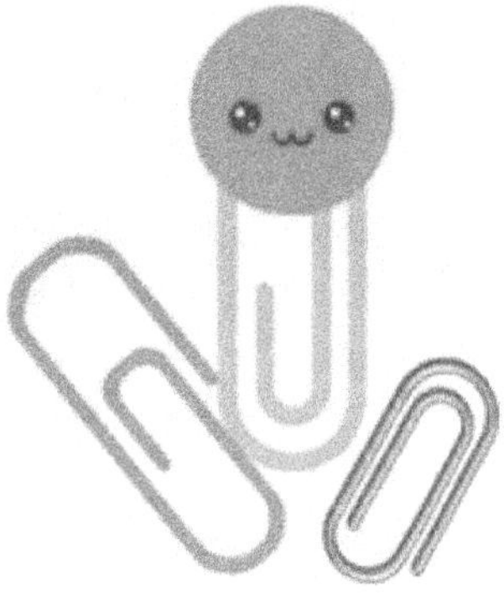

Clips can hold up paper.

papier

paper

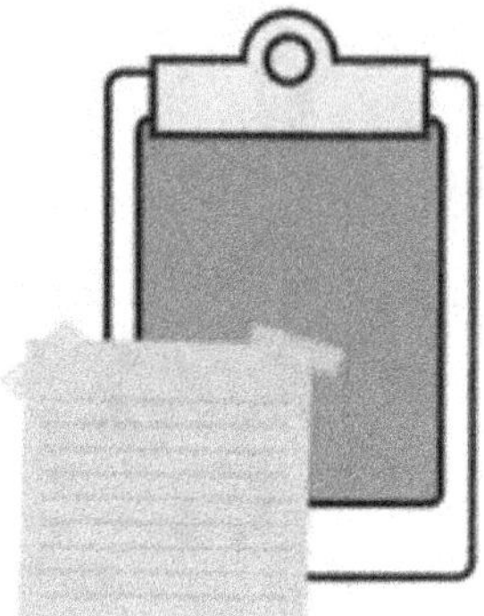

I have lots of paper.

agrafeuse

stapler

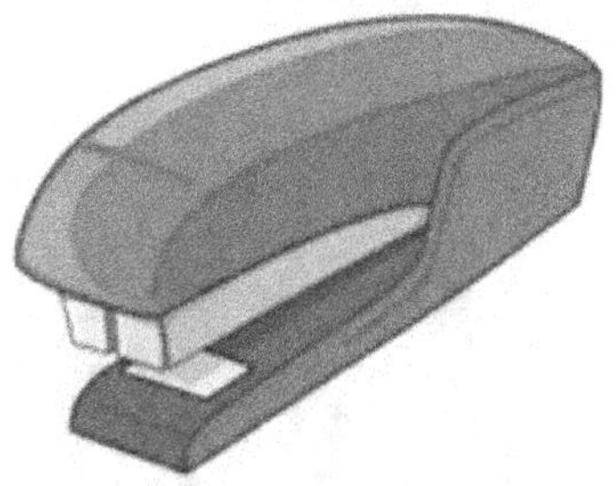

My stapler is shiny and red.

calculatrice

calculator

My calculator has buttons.

règle

ruler

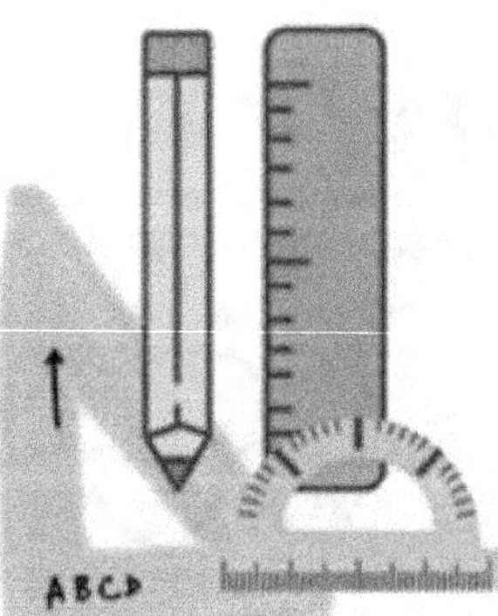

I have lots of rulers.

la colle

glue

The glue is sticky.

bibliothèque

bookcase

My bookcase has lots of things.

calendrier

calendar

I have a calendar on my table.

chaise

chair

My chair is fancy.

l'horloge

clock

The clock says that it's 3 o'clock.

ordinateur

computer

I do things on my computer.

bureaux

desk

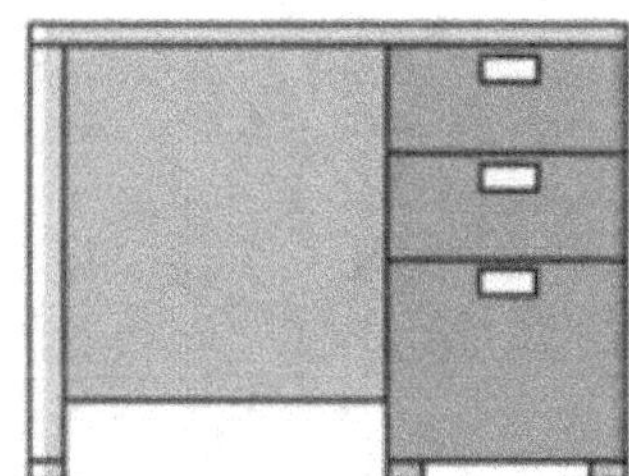

I put lots of things on my desk.

dictionnaire

dictionary

The dictionary has lots of words.

la gomme

eraser

Erasers are used with pencils.

carte

map

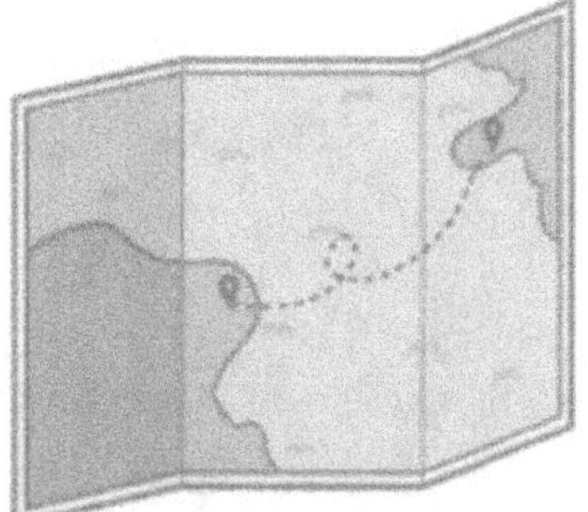

The map shows you different places.

carnet

notebook

I use notebooks at school.

stylo

pen

My pen is very pretty.

crayon

pencil

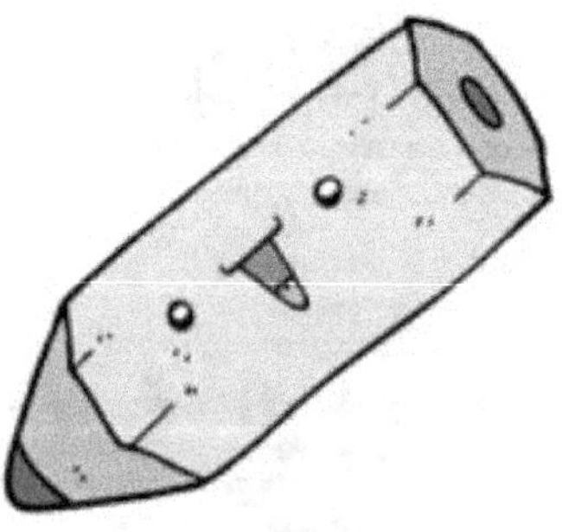

My friend gave me a pencil.

ceinture

belt

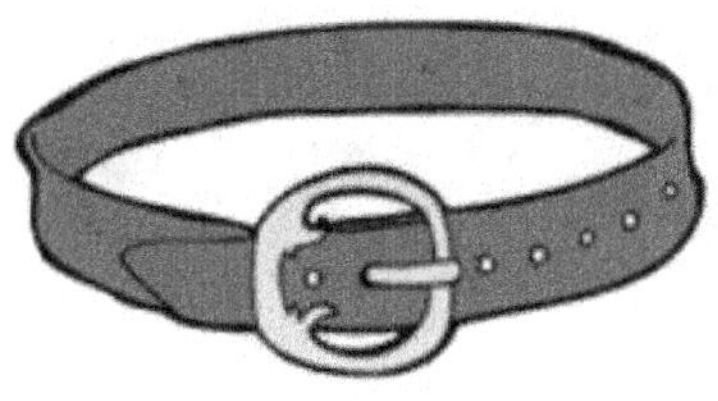

I have a belt on my pants.

bottes

boots

I have big brown boots.

chapeau

cap

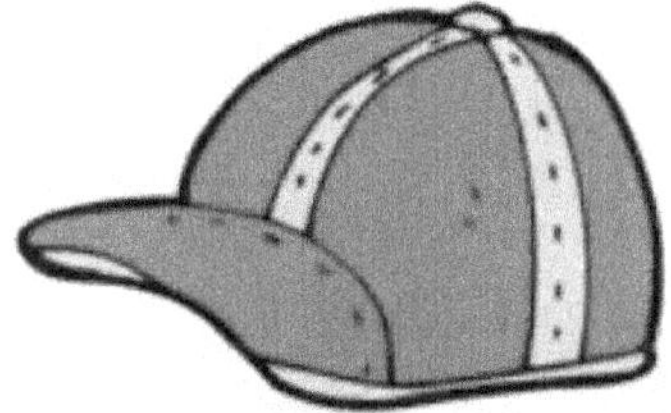

My mom bought me a new cap.

manteau

coat

She has a long yellow coat.

robes

dress

My dress has a bow.

gants

gloves

I got new gloves.

chapeau

hat

That hat is for a wicked witch.

veste

jacket

The jacket is cozy.

jeans

jeans

My jeans are long.

pyjamas

pajamas

I sleep in my pajamas.

un pantalon

pants

The bear is wearing pants.

imperméable

raincoat

We wear our raincoats when it is raining.

écharpe

scarf

The baby has a scarf around his neck.

chemise

shirt

I like this shirt the best.

des chaussures

shoes

I have red and blue shoes.

jupe

skirt

My skirt has lots of buttons.

pantalon

slacks

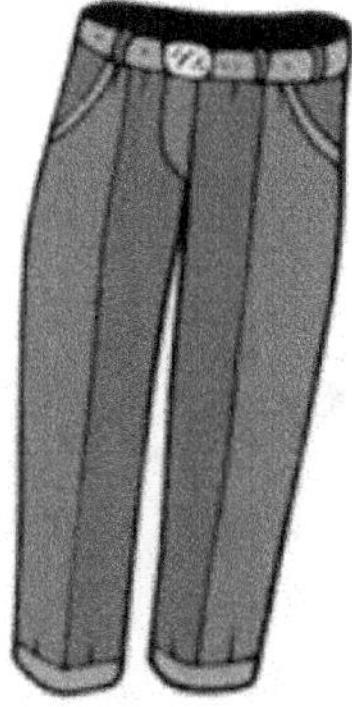

My dad wears slacks.

chaussons

slippers

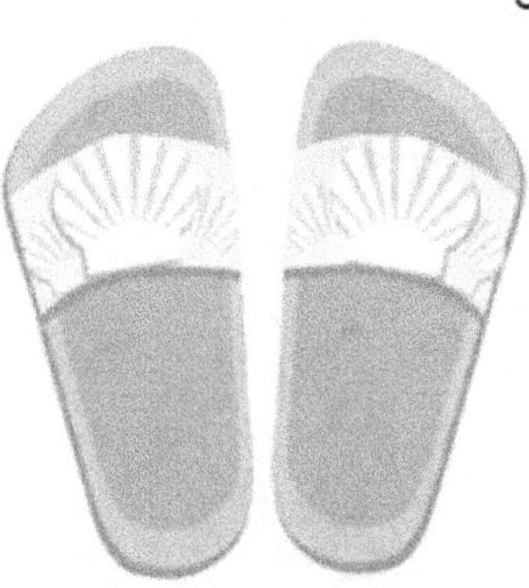

I have seashells on my sandals.

chaussettes

socks

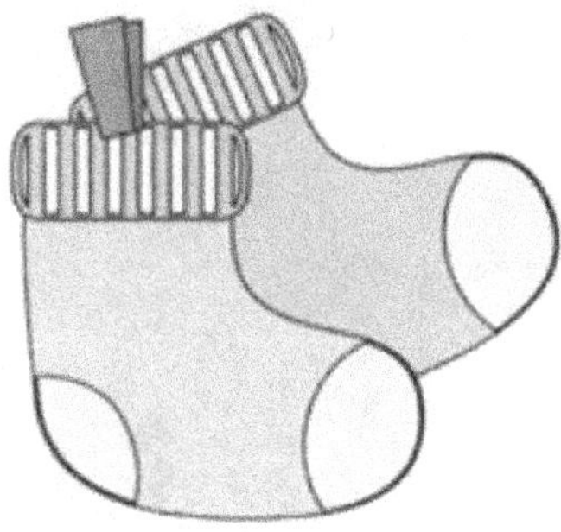

My baby sister wears socks.

costume

suit

My brother is wearing a suit.

chandail

sweater

I am wearing a sweater for winter.

cravate

tie

My dad wears a tie to meetings.

pantalon

trousers

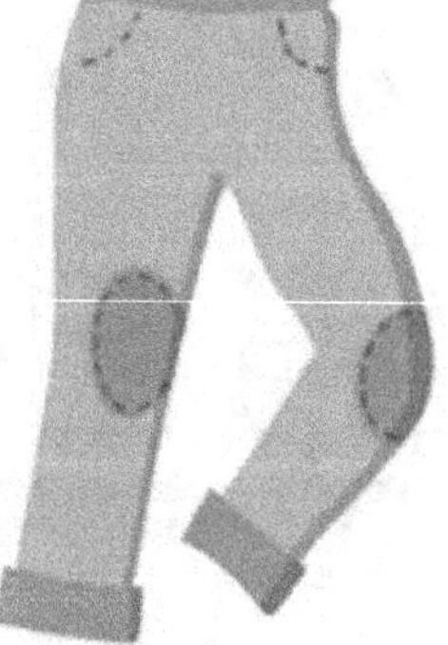

The trousers look like jeans.

slip

underpants

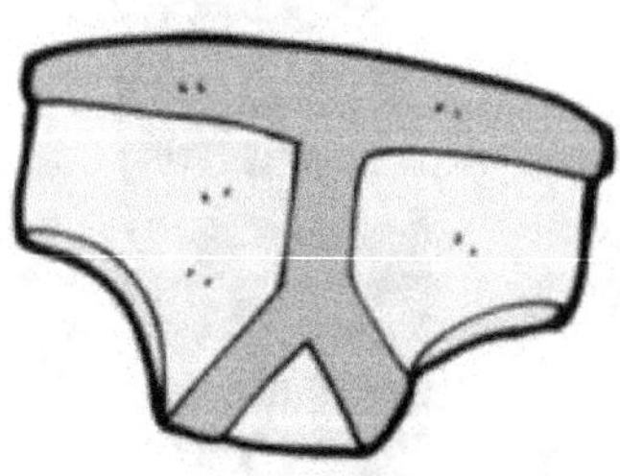

I always wear my underwear.

maillot de corps

undershirt

My undershirt has a star.

une

one

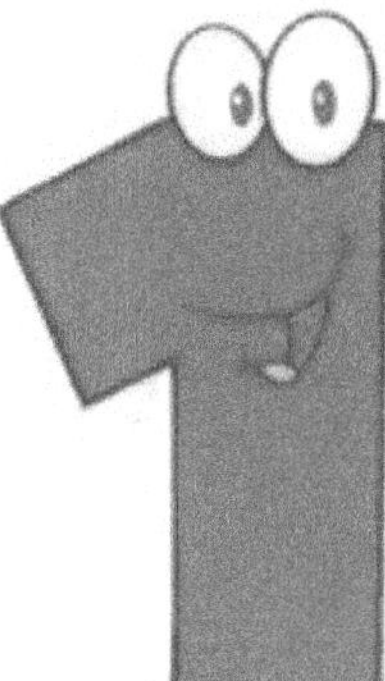

Number one and the bee are friends.

deux

two

The cat and the mouse both love two.

trois

three

The bear gives number three a present.

quatre

four

Number four is a home for the cat.

cinq

five

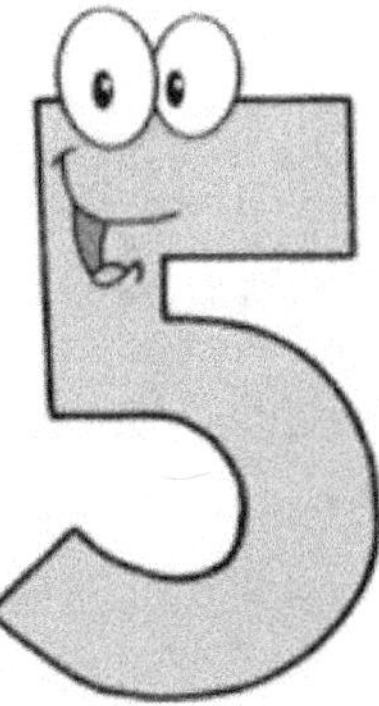

Number five hatches an egg.

six

six

Number six is going to eat a carrot.

sept

seven

Number seven is playing with the tiger.

huit

eight

Number eight is funny.

neuf

nine

Number nine meets the parrot.

dix

ten

Number ten is smiling.

onze

eleven

Number eleven has big eyes.

douze

twelve

Number twelve is number one and two.

treize

thirteen

Number thirteen is excited.

quatorze

fourteen

The number fourteen is vast.

quinze

fifteen

The number fifteen is green.

seize

sixteen

Sixteen is my lucky number.

dix-sept

seventeen

Number seventeen look alike.

dix-huit

eighteen

Number eighteen will go to the circus.

dix-neuf

nineteen

I am nineteen now!

vingt

twenty

Number twenty has a zero.

fourmi

ant

The ant has lots of legs.

cloche

bell

The bell will ring.

vache

cow

The cow has a bow.

poupée

doll

She has a cute bear doll.

oeuf

egg

The chick has hatched out of the egg.

poisson

fish

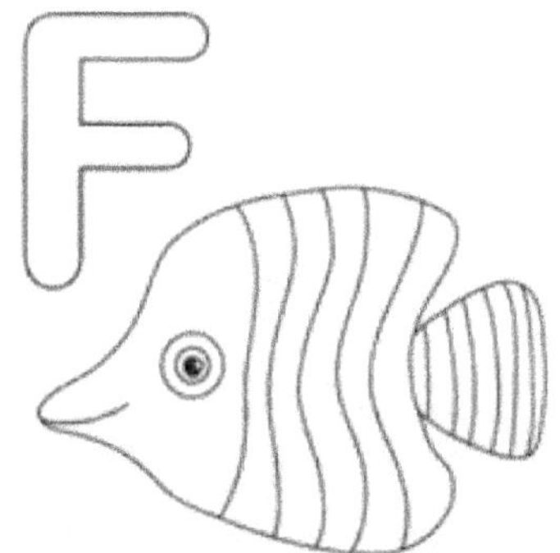

The fish is swimming in the water.

chèvre

goat

The goat is sitting on the grass.

chapeau

hat

He is wearing a hat.

crème glacée

ice cream

I like to eat ice cream.

confiture

jam

The kitten is sitting on the jam jar.

chaton

kitten

The cat is sleeping on the floor.

lion

lion

The lion is waiting for the tiger.

rat

mouse

The mouse has lots of presents.

nez

nose

The reindeer has a red nose.

hibou

owl

The owl is sleeping.

porc

pig

The pig will eat cupcakes.

reine

queen

The queen has a big crown.

lapin

rabbit

The rabbit is jumping up and down.

mouton

sheep

The sheep have fluffy wool.

tortue

turtle

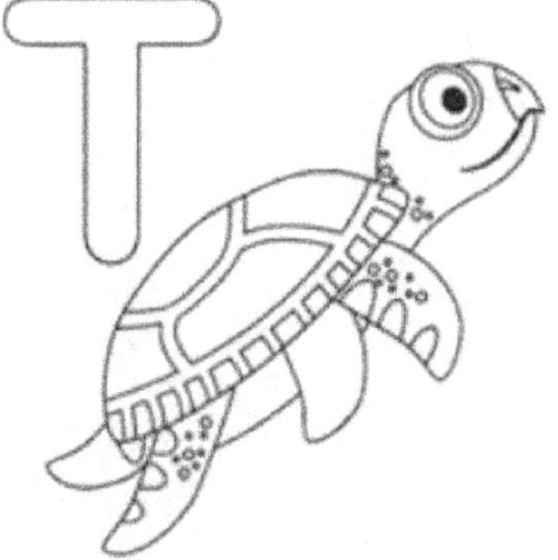

The turtle has a shell.

parapluie

umbrella

The mouse is holding an umbrella.

van

van

The van is driving along the road.

pastèque

watermelon

The watermelon has lots of seeds.

xylophone

xylophone

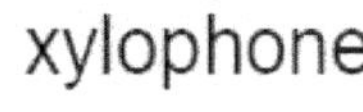

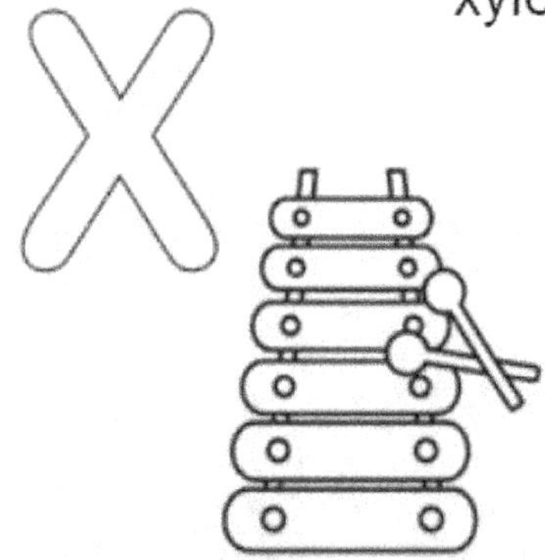

We are going to play the xylophone.

yaourt

yogurt

We opened the yogurt can.

zèbre

zebra

The zebra is surprised.

rose

pink

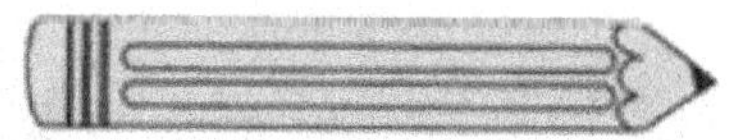

color the word and
the picture in pink

Most of my clothes are pink.

marron

brown

color the word and
the picture in pink

My chocolate is brown.

gris

gray

color the word and
the picture in pink

I don't like the color gray.

vert

green

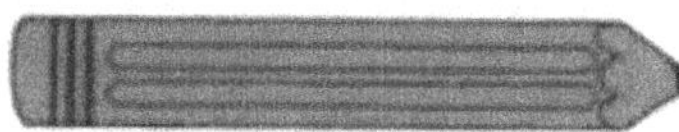

color the word and
the picture in pink

The vegetables are green.

jaune

yellow

color the word and
the picture in pink

Bananas are yellow.

blanc

white

color the word and
the picture in pink

The paper that I write on is white.

rouge

red

color the word and
the picture in pink

Apples are red.

bleu

blue

color the word and the picture in pink

The night sky is blue.

percer

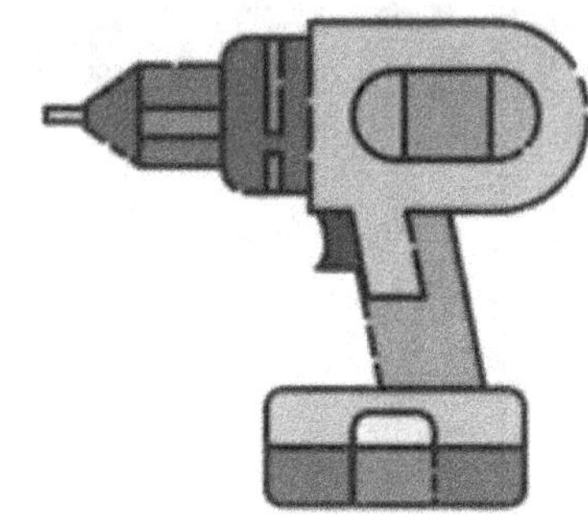

drill

The drill will help us fix this.

marteau

hammer

The hammer is going to nail the picture.

couteau

knife

The knife is sharp.

pinces

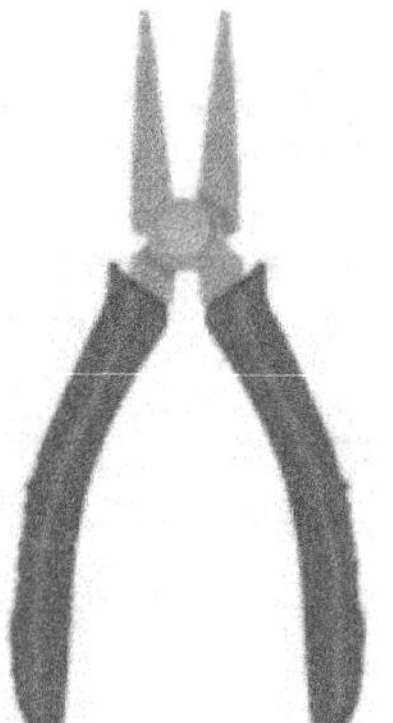

pliers

The plier is used for many things.

vu

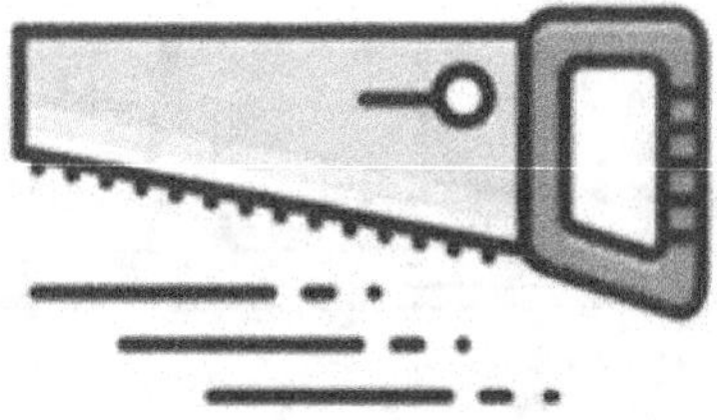

saw

The saw can chop wood.

les ciseaux

scissors

I use scissors to cut paper.

tournevis

screwdriver

The screwdriver can screw in the knots.

clé

wrench

The wrench can help unscrew the knots.

avion

airplane

The airplane is going to leave now.

vélo

bicycle

The bicycle is beautiful.

bateau

boat

The boat is floating on the water.

autobus

bus

The bus is going to school.

voiture

car

The car is green.

hélicoptère

helicopter

The helicopter is looking for something.

cheval

horse

You can ride the horse.

jet

jet

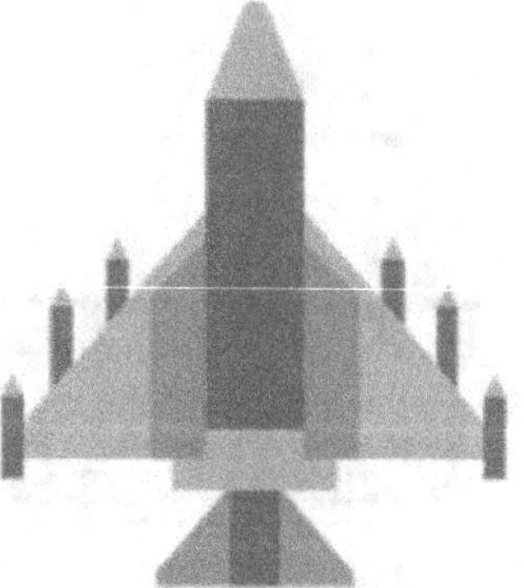

The jet is high-speed.

moto

motorcycle

The motorcycle is on the road.

navire

ship

The ship is on the water.

métro

subway

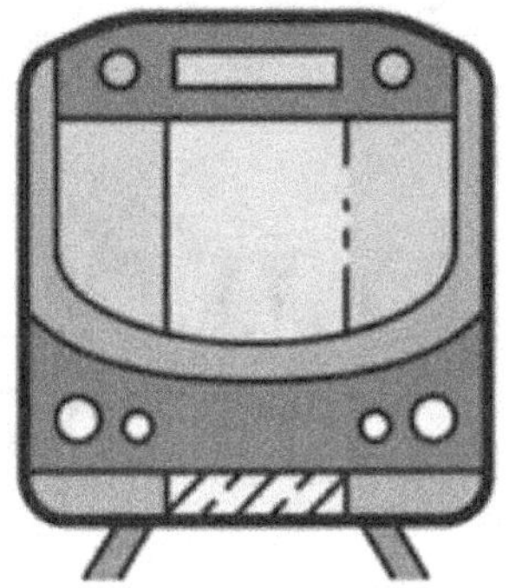

My mom goes on the subway to work.

taxi

taxi

The taxi has someone inside.

train

train

The train is going slowly.

un camion

truck

The truck has stuff in it.

asperges

asparagus

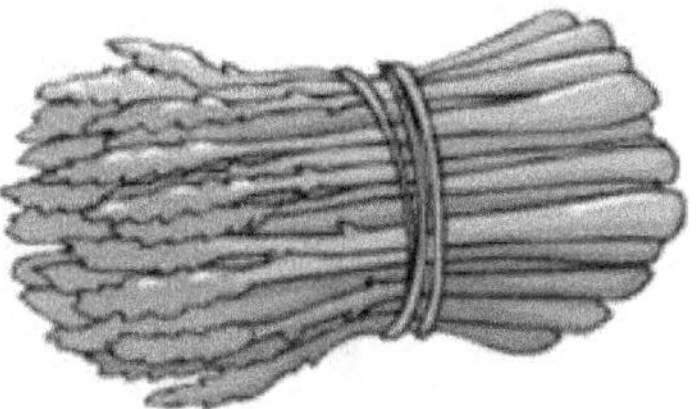

The asparagus is in a bundle.

des haricots

beans

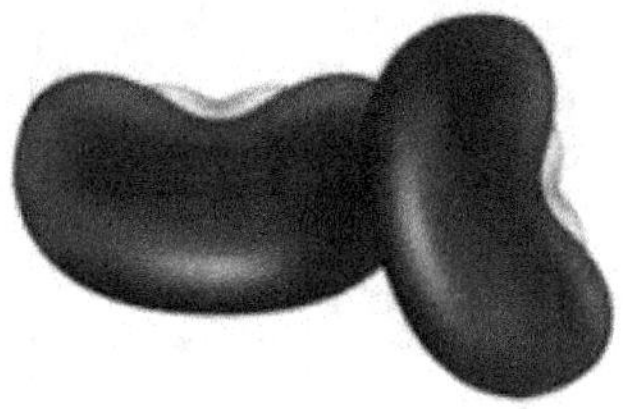

The beans are smooth.

brocoli

broccoli

The broccoli is dancing.

chou

cabbage

Bunnies like to eat cabbage.

carotte

carrot

The carrots are very long.

céleri

celery

The celery has lots of leaves.

blé

corn

Corn soup is delicious.

concombre

cucumber

The cucumbers are cut into pieces.

aubergine

eggplant

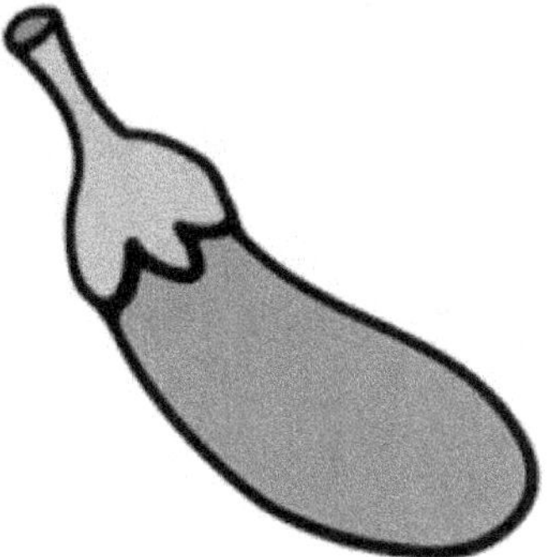

The eggplant is purple.

poivre vert

green pepper

The green pepper is juicy.

salade

lettuce

The lettuce is all green.

oignon

onion

The onions make my eyes water.

pois

peas

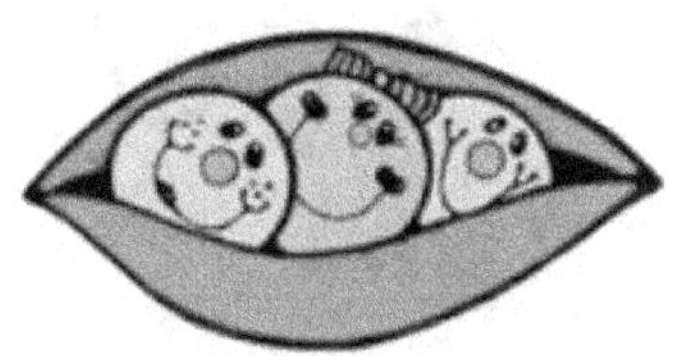

The peas are all in a pod.

patate

potato

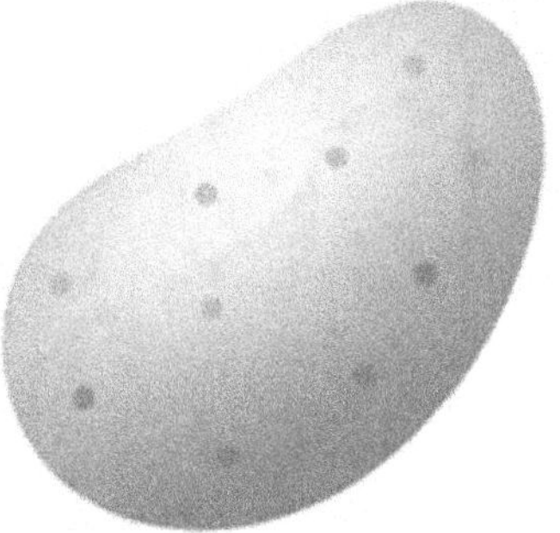

The potato is very shiny.

citrouille

pumpkin

The pumpkin is for Halloween.

un radis

radish

The radish is a type of vegetable.

épinard

spinach

The spinach is good with cheese.

patate douce

sweet potato

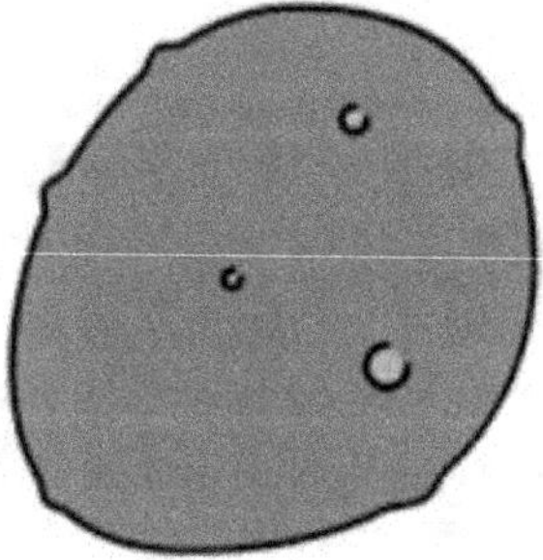

The sweet potato is quite sweet.

tomate

tomato

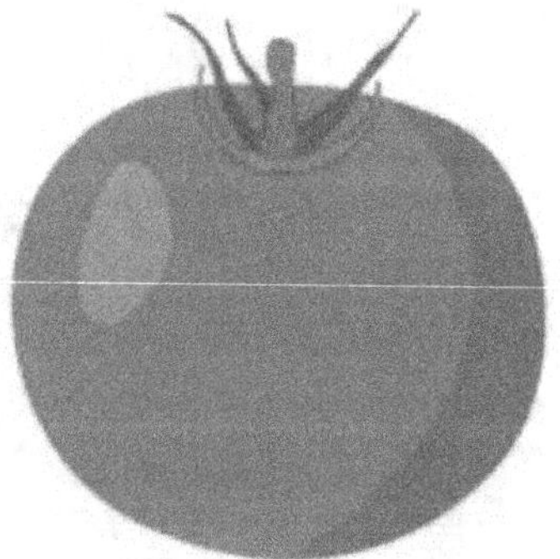

I don't like to eat tomatoes.

navet

turnip

My mom bought some turnips.

nuageux

cloudy

The weather is cloudy today.

du froid

cold

I like cold weather.

cool

cool

The temperature is cold today.

brumeux

foggy

The fog is so strong I can't see the city.

chaud

hot

The fire is burning hot.

humide

humid

It's so humid and wet today.

pluvieux

rainy

It's raining very hard.

neigeux

snowy

Welcome to snow land!

orageux

stormy

I hate the stormy weather.

ensoleillé

sunny

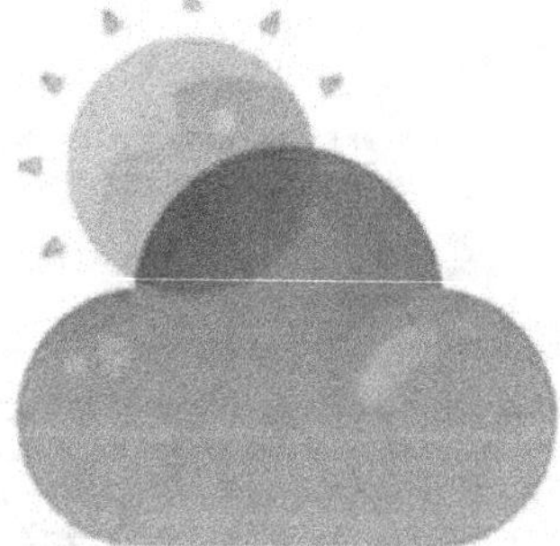

The sun is shining!

chaud

warm

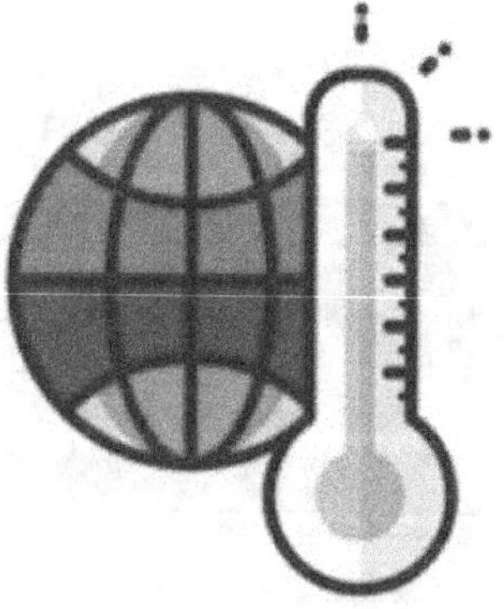

The whole world is warm today!

venteux

windy

The leaves are blowing away since it's so windy!

tante

aunt

My aunt is very nice to me.

frère

brother

My brother is very fun to play with.

cousin

cousin

I love going to the playground with my cousin.

fille

daughter

I like to read books with my daughter.

père

father

My father is playing with me.

petite fille

granddaughter

My granddaughter has blond hair.

grand-mère

grandmother

My grandmother is very old and has glasses.

petit fils

grandson

My grandson and I are very excited today!

mère

mother

My mother likes to pick me up.

neveu

nephew

My father's nephew is my cousin.

nièce

niece

My niece is very good at playing ball.

sœur

sister

My sister is so pretty!

fils

son

My son likes to play with toy cars.

belle fille

stepdaughter

My stepdaughter likes the color orange.

belle-mère

stepmother

My stepmother is pretty.

beau-fils

stepson

This is my stepson, Greg.

oncle

uncle

My uncle tells lots of funny jokes.

bol

bowl

The bowl has nothing inside.

tasse

cup

My mom drinks her coffee out of a cup.

plat

dish

That dish has a bone inside.

fourchette

fork

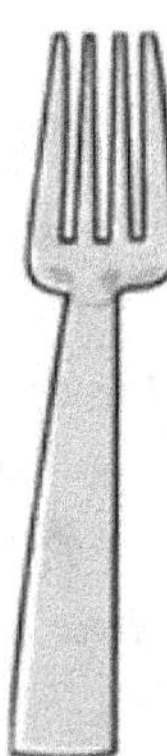

We have more spoons than forks.

verre

glass

I have a glass of water on my desk.

couteau

knife

I have a knife in my kitchen.

agresser

mug

This mug of coffee is for my dad.

serviette de table

napkin

You can use the napkins to clean your hands.

poivre

pepper

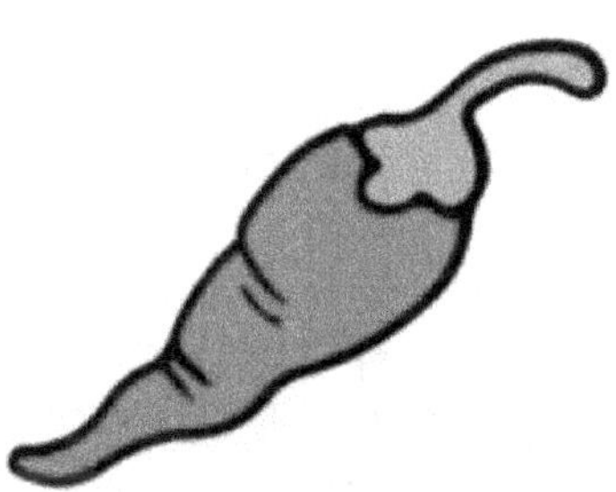

The pepper is very spicy.

lanceur

pitcher

Pour yourself some lemonade from the pitcher.

assiette

plate

Can you help me wash the plates?

salade

salad

The salad is very healthy for you.

sel

salt

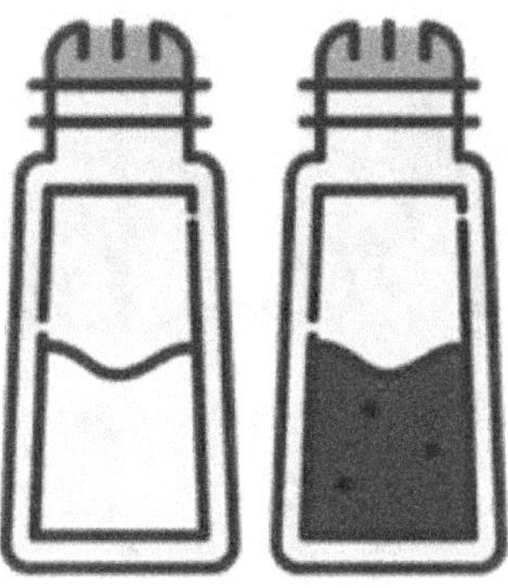

The salt tastes good with a few pinches of pepper.

soucoupe

saucer

The plate is for my cup.

cuillère

spoon

I use a spoon to eat my rice.

sucre

sugar

The pack of sugar is very heavy.

dimanche

Sunday

Sunday

Sunday is the day to go to Church!

lundi

Monday

Monday

Monday is the day to start school.

<table>
<tr><td>

mardi

Tuesday

Tuesday

We will go to the shops on Tuesday.

</td><td>

mercredi

Wednesday

Wednesday

Wednesday is hard to spell!

</td></tr>
<tr><td>

jeudi

Thursday

Thursday

Thursday is the fourth day of the week!

</td><td>

vendredi

Friday

Friday

My birthday is on Friday!

</td></tr>
<tr><td>

samedi

Saturday

Saturday

Saturday is the weekend!

</td><td>

cuire

bake

The chef will bake a cake.

</td></tr>
</table>

ébullition

boil

I will boil the eggs.

griller

broil

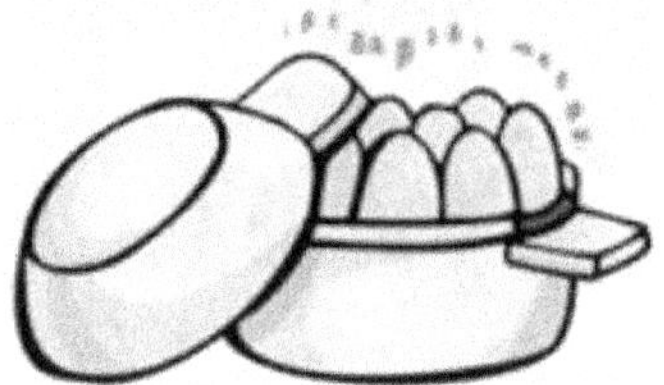

Broil is very yummy.

ouvre-boîte

can opener

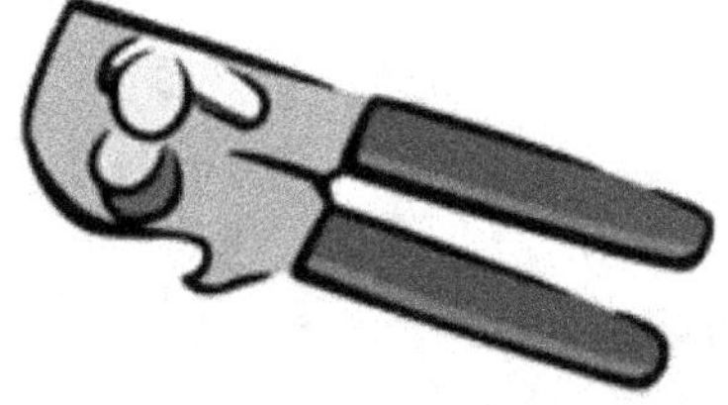

That can opener is used for opening cans.

frire

fry

The pan can fry lots of things.

gril

grill

We have a grill in our backyard.

tasse à mesurer

measuring cup

My mom uses the measuring cup for baking.

cuillère à mesurer

measuring spoon

I use a measuring spoon to eat my dessert.

four micro onde

microwave

The microwave is used to heat food.

bol à mélanger

mixing bowl

She is using the mixing bowl to mix things.

serviettes en papier

paper towels

Dry your hands with paper towels.

poché aux œufs

poach

The poach is put on noodles.

porte pot

potholder

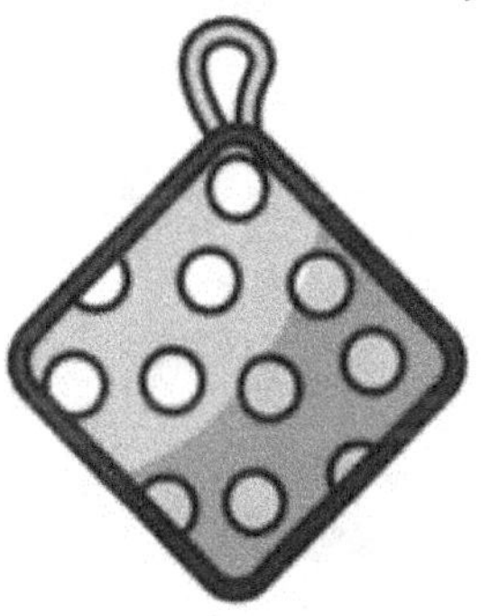

The potholder is soft.

rôti

roast

The chef made roast chicken.

rouleau à pâtisserie

rolling pin

He is holding a rolling pin.

brouiller

scramble

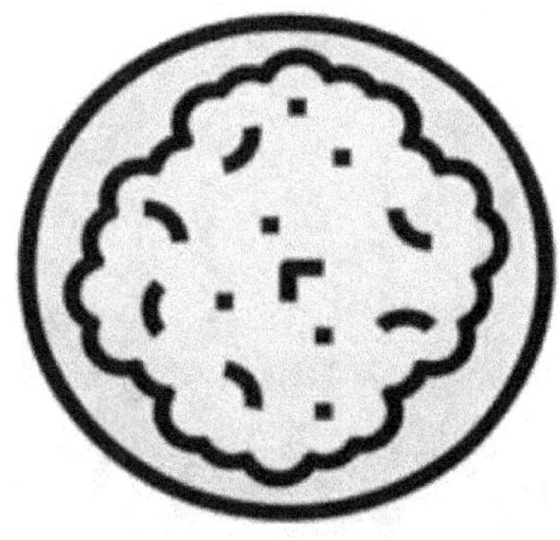

My mom is making scrambled eggs for breakfast.

mijoter

simmer

The simmer is rice today.

couteau

knife

The knife is sharp.

cuillère

spoon

I eat my food with a spoon and fork.

spatule

spatula

The spatula will help us flip the steak over.

vapeur

steam

The steam is coming from the pot.

passoire

strainer

The strainer is used to strain stuff.

minuteur

timer

I set my timer for 12:00.

fourchette

fork

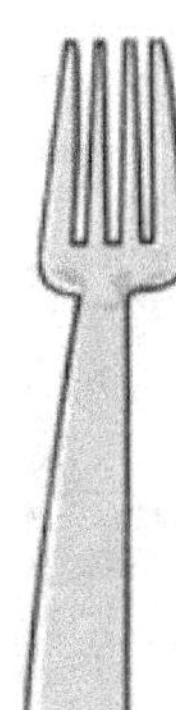

I have lots of metallic forks.

grille-pain

toaster

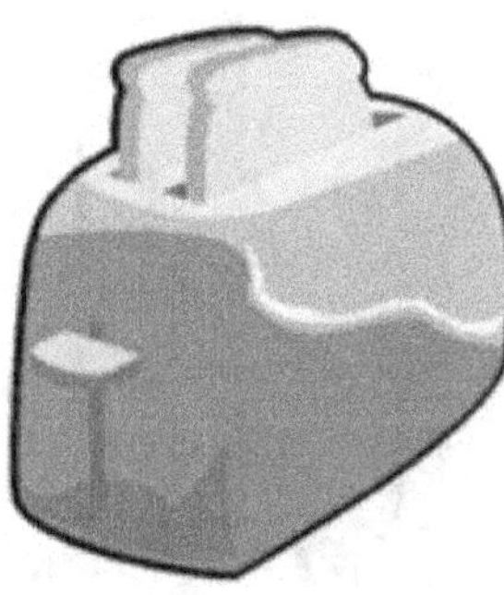

The toaster will toast my bread.

bouilloire

kettle

The kettle has tea inside.

réfrigérateur

refrigerator

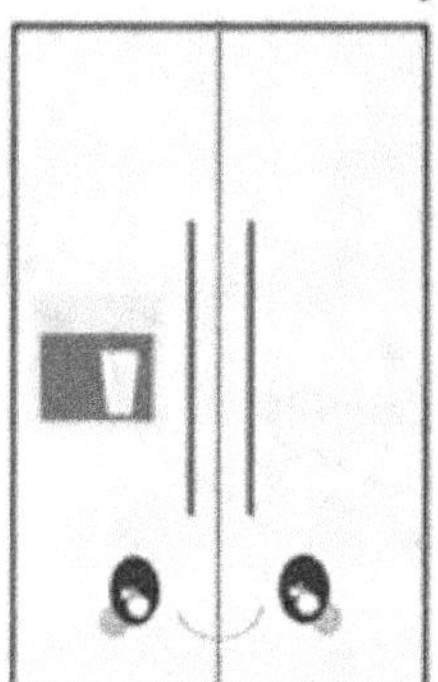

The refrigerator has lots of things inside.

mixeur

blender

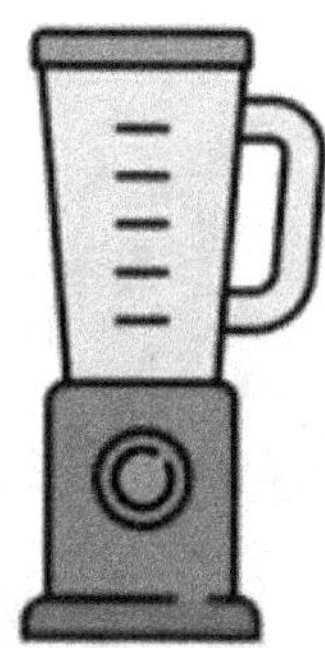

The blender will mix up my fruits.

cabinets

cabinet

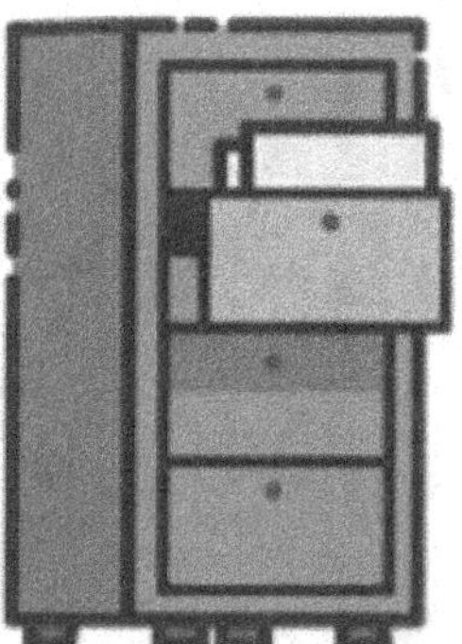

The cabinet has my paper inside.

placard

cupboard

The cupboard has lots of books.

four micro onde

microwave

The microwave will heat my food.

arrière

back

She has a slender back.

des joues

cheeks

She kisses her mom on the cheek.

poitrine

chest

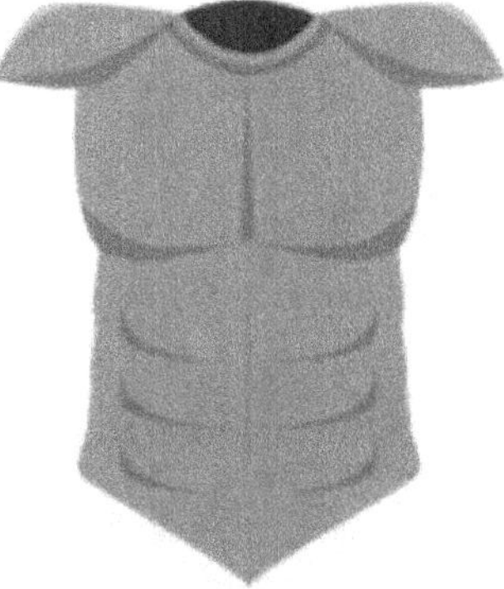

The armor is for your chest.

menton

chin

This is my chin!

oreilles

ears

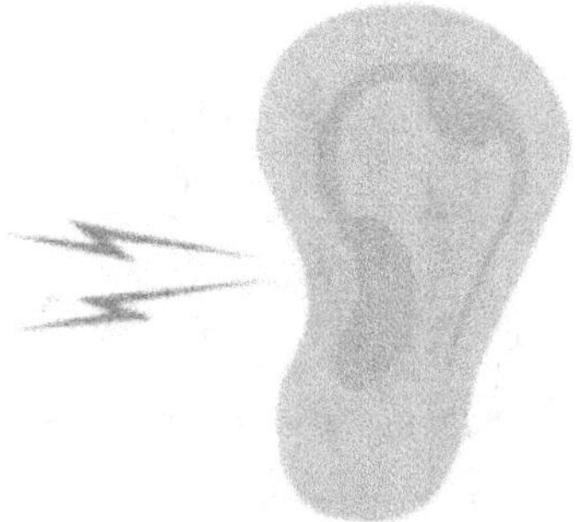

The ear is hearing something.

les sourcils

eyebrows

The eyebrows are raised.

yeux

eyes

The eyes are blue.

pieds

feet

I have one pair of feet.

des doigts

fingers

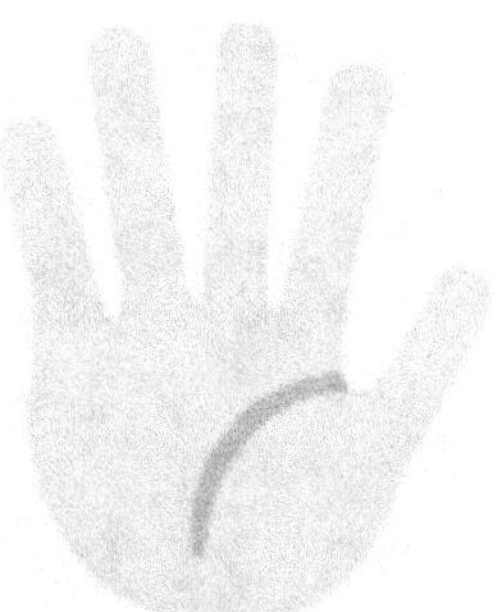

The fingers are waving at us.

pied

foot

My foot has five fingers.

front

forehead

My brain is behind my forehead.

cheveux

hair

My hair is long and black.

mains

hands

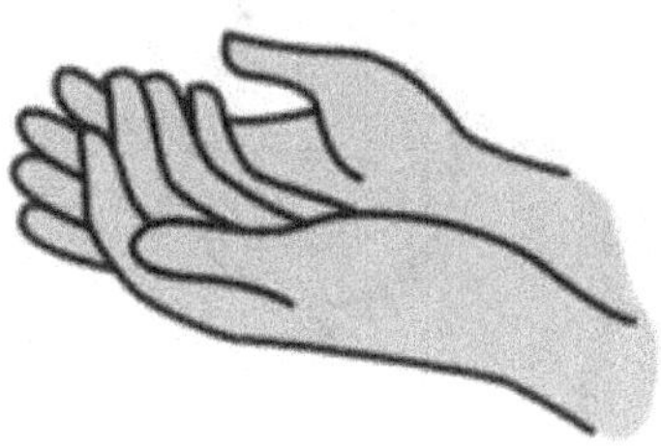

I will wash my hands in the sink.

tête

head

She has a big head.

les hanches

hips

The gorilla has his hands on his hips.

les genoux

knees

She is begging on her knees.

jambes

legs

The tiger has strong legs.

lèvres

lips

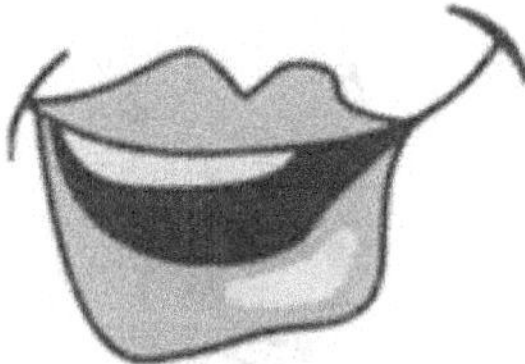

The lips have lipstick on.

bouche

mouth

He is covering his mouth with his hand.

cou

neck

The necklace is very special to me.

nez

nose

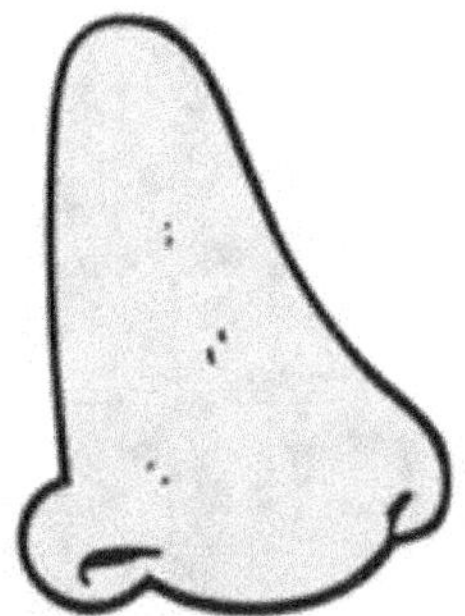

The nose smells something.

épaules

shoulders

He puts his hands on his shoulders.

estomac

stomach

He has a big stomach.

les dents

teeth

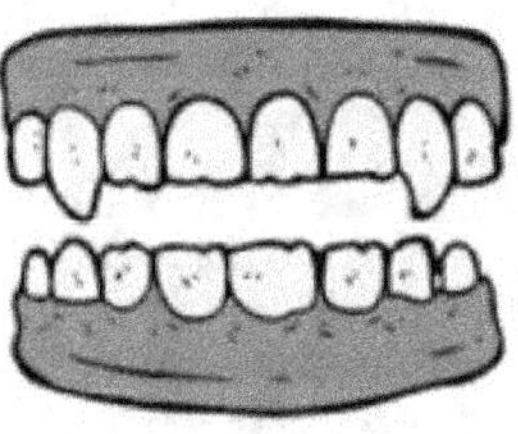

The teeth are clean and white.

gorge

throat

He has a sore throat today.

les orteils

toes

My toes are small.

langue

tongue

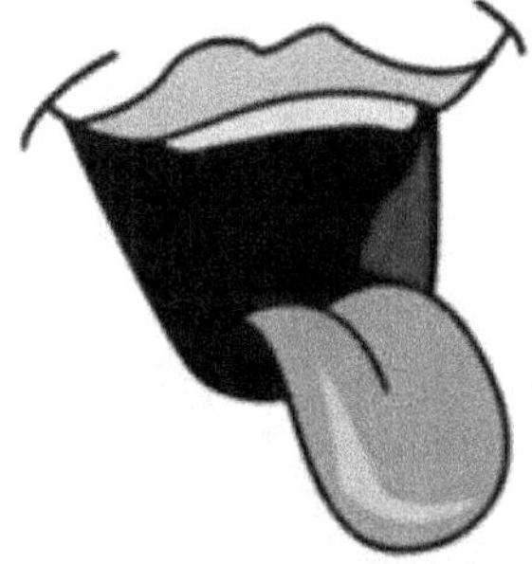

My tongue is licking ice cream.

dent

tooth

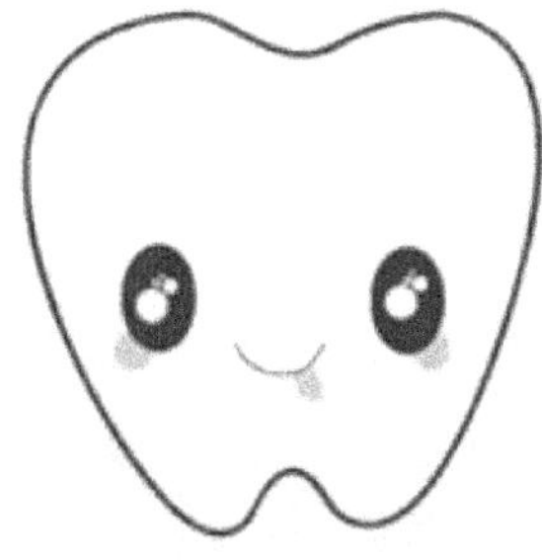

The tooth has big eyes.

taille

waist

He has his hands on his waist.

salopette

overalls

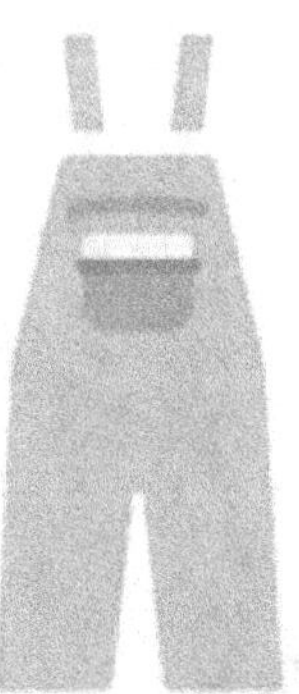

I bought these overalls for you!

mitaines

mittens

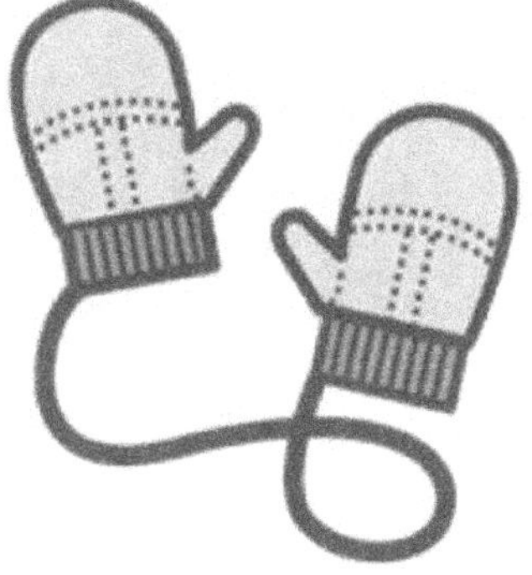

The mittens are very warm.

bonnet

beanie

The beanie is for winter.

tablier

apron

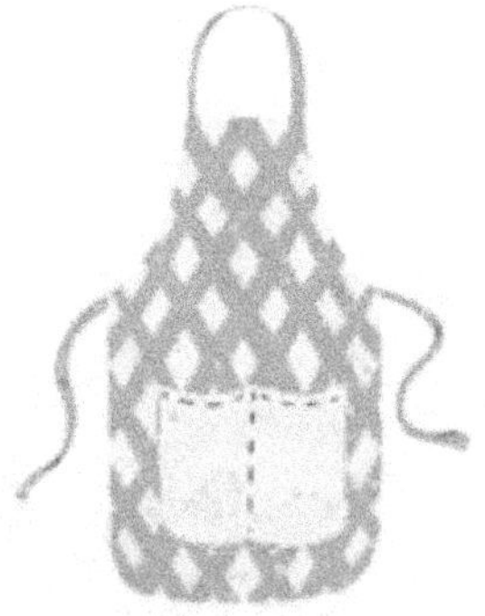

I wear my apron when I bake.

poupée

doll

The doll is for my baby sister.

hochets

rattle

The rattle is for the baby.

jouet

toy

The toy is very fun.

couche

diaper

The baby has to wear a diaper.

berceau

bassinet

She is sleeping in her bassinet.

bavoir

bib

My baby brother has to wear his bib when he is eating.

octogone

octagon

The octagon is saying okay!

triangle

triangle

The triangle has three corners.

carré

square

Square

The square has four sides.

cercle

circle

Circle

The circle is round.

ovale

oval

The oval shape looks like a circle.

cœur

heart

I drew a heart on my paper.

traverser

cross

That sign is a cross.

la flèche

arrow

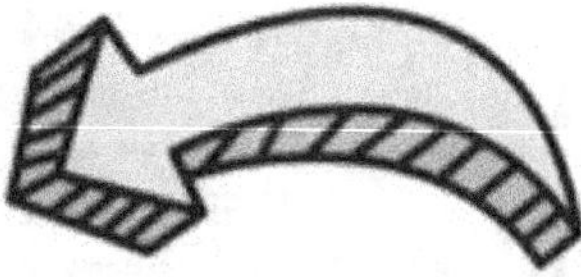

The arrow is pointing this way.

cube

cube

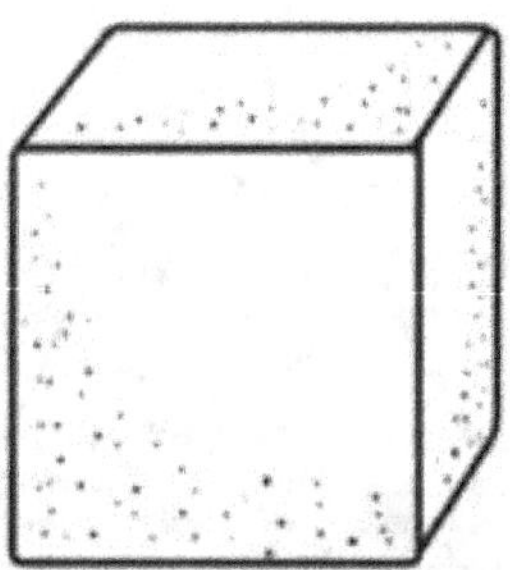

The cube is 3D.

étoile

star

The star is yellow and shiny.

tir à l'arc

archery

The archery is where you aim.

badminton

badminton

My favorite sport is badminton.

criquet

cricket

I am very good at cricket.

bowling

bowling

I got one pin down at bowling!

boxe

boxing

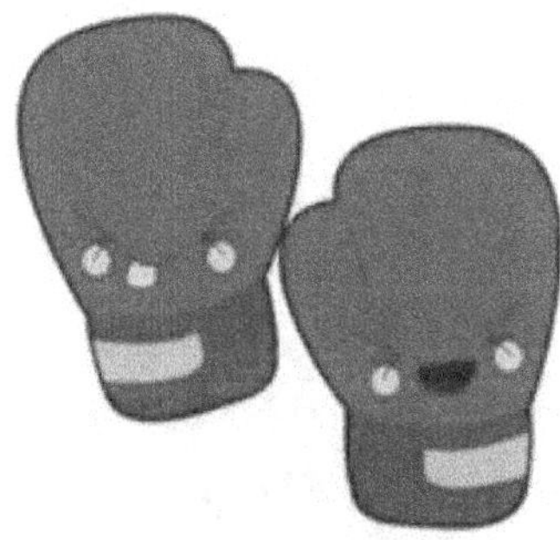

The boxing gloves are hot.

tennis

tennis

He can hit the ball in tennis.

faire de la planche a roulettes

skateboarding

He skateboards to school.

planche de surf

surfing

The shark loves surfing in the ocean.

le hockey

hockey

I like to play Ice hockey.

yoga

yoga

He is closing his eyes and doing yoga.

épée

fencing

They are fencing and dueling together.

aptitude

fitness

She will do some fitness in the pool.

gymnastique

gymnastics

He can do brilliant gymnastics.

karaté

karate

She is good at kicking in Karate.

volley-ball

volleyball

She is holding a volleyball.

musculation

weightlifting

The girl with brown hair can do weightlifting.

basketball

basketball

He can balance the ball with one finger in basketball.

base-ball

baseball

The little chick is in the finales at baseball.

le rugby

rugby

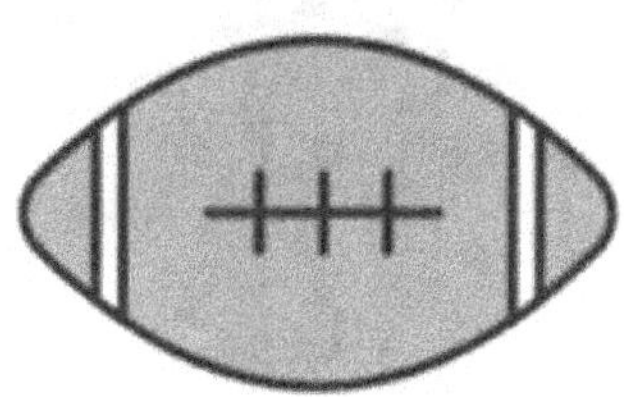

The rugby ball has white stripes.

lutte

wrestling

The sumo will compete in wrestling.

course de voitures

car racing

He is number one for car racing.

cyclisme

cycling

He is peacefully cycling on the road.

fonctionnement

running

He is running while listening to his earphones.

tennis de table

table tennis

My brother and dad will play table tennis.

pêche

fishing

He will go to the river to fish.

judo

judo

She has a red belt in Judo.

escalade

climbing

He will climb the ladder.

tournage

shooting

He is shooting the archery board.

le golf

golf

She is going to compete in the golf competition.

balade

ride

He will ride his scooter.

asseyez-vous

sit down

They are sitting down together.

se lever

stand up

She likes to stand up.

bats toi

fight

They are fighting over the book.

rire

laugh

He is laughing so hard!

lis

read

She read a picture book.

jouer

play

He went to play on the slide.

ecoutez

listen

He listened for the ice cream cart.

pleurer

cry

He cried because he got a bad grade.

pense

think

He thought that the test would be hard.

chanter

sing

He sang for the concert.

regarder la télévision

watch tv

He watched TV the whole night.

danse

dance

She was a good dancer.

allumer

turn on

The light is turned on.

éteindre

turn off

The light is turned off.

gagner

win

He won the contest.

mouche

fly

The parrot can fly.

couper

cut

He was cutting his nails.

désinvolte

throw away

He threw away the garbage.

dormir

sleep

He slept soundly.

fermer

close

He closed his mouth shut.

ouvert

open

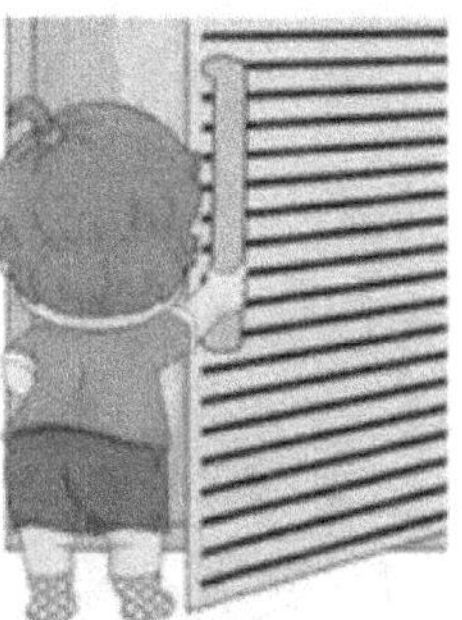

She opened the bathroom door.

écrire

write

She wrote with a pencil.

donner

give

Santa gave her a present.

sauter

jump

She had fun jumping.

manger

eat

The shark ate yummy ice cream.

boisson

drink

The old British man drank tea.

cuisinier

cook

The microwave cooked his soup.

lavage

wash

You need to remember to wash your hands.

attendre

wait

He was waiting for the bus.

montée

climb

She climbed a lot of mountains.

parler

talk

Two best friends were talking together.

crawl

crawl

The baby crawled on the floor.

rêver

dream

The Sloth dreamed about eating leaves.

creuser

dig

That strong man dug a swimming pool.

taper

clap

The baby clapped her hands.

tricoter

knit

She knits with the purple string.

coudre

sew

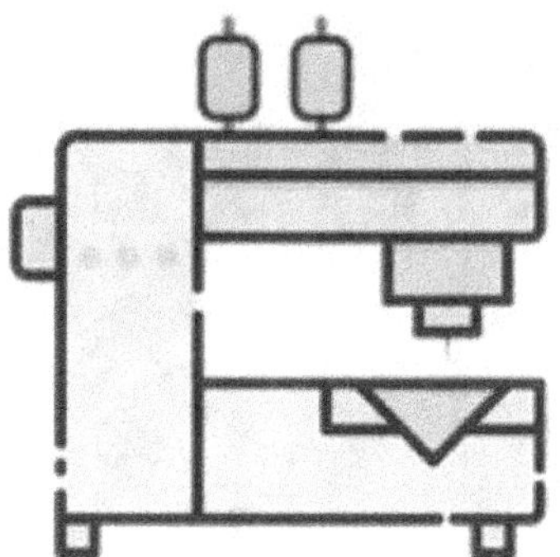

That is a sewing machine.

odeur

smell

The perfume smelled great.

baiser

kiss

He kissed his mother.

étreinte

hug

They hugged each other.

ronfler

snore

The tiger snored.

baigner

bathe

He took a bath.

s'incliner

bow

He bowed to the judge.

peindre

paint

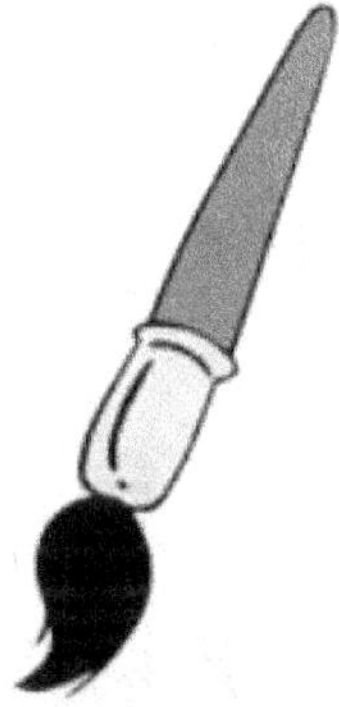

He painted a colorful picture.

se plonger

dive

He dove to the deepest part of the ocean.

ski

ski

The ski was expensive.

empiler

stack

The books are stacked high.

acheter

buy

They bought cereal.

secouer

shake

They shook hands together.

programmeur

programmer

He was a smart computer programmer.

vétérinaire

veterinarian

She is a veterinarian.

vendeur de rue

street vendor

That street vendor sells hot dogs.

mineur

miner

That Miner will find gold.

prof

teacher

The owl is the teacher.

groom

bellboy

That Bellboy is fat.

orateur

speaker

The chicken is a great Speaker.

boucher

butcher

The Butcher sells fish.

pharmacien

pharmacist

That Pharmacist saved a person's life.

réceptionniste

receptionist

He is a Receptionist.

politicien

politician

He wants to be a Politician.

guide touristique

tour guide

That Tour guide led us around Japan.

entrepreneur

entrepreneur

He is an Entrepreneur.

danseuse de ballet

ballet dancer

She is training to be a Ballet dancer.

astronaute

astronaut

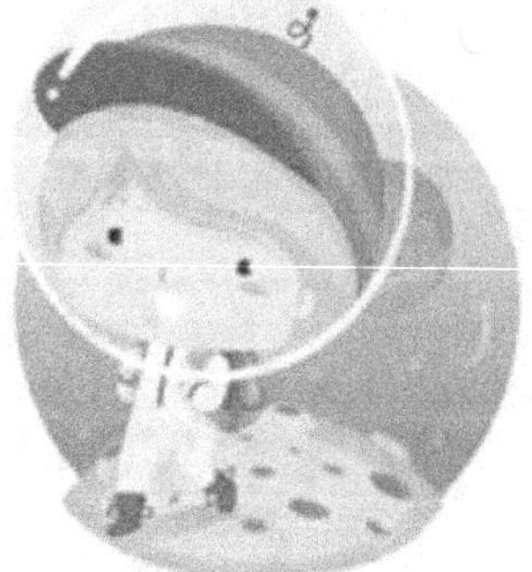

He is a great astronaut.

juge

judge

That Judge is always fair.

avocat

lawyer

The lawyer is serious.

la caissière

cashier

She is a cashier at the market.

conducteur de taxi

taxi driver

He is a fast Taxi driver.

plombier

plumber

That Plumber fixes toilets.

musicien

musician

She wants to be a Musician like her teacher.

chef

chef

The chef makes fast food.

boulanger

baker

That baker is a bread.

artiste

artist

That Artist came from Italy.

acteur

actor

That actor is famous.

barman

bartender

The Bartender works in a bar.

coiffeur

hairdresser

That girl is a Hairdresser.

évêques

bishop

He is a Bishop.

opticien

optician

She went to an Optician.

fleuriste

florist

She is a great Florist.

écrivain

writer

He is a famous author.

comptable

accountant

My accountant is loyal.

du vin

wine

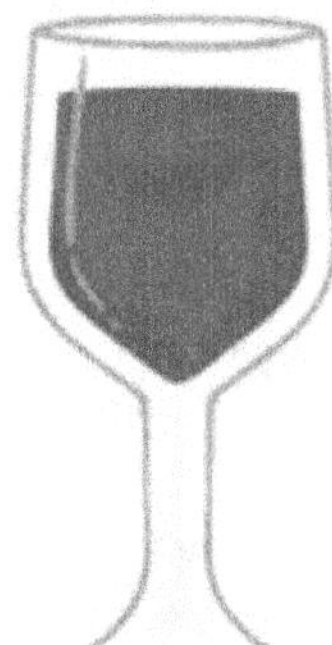

That wine tastes good.

café

coffee

That coffee is bitter.

limonade

lemonade

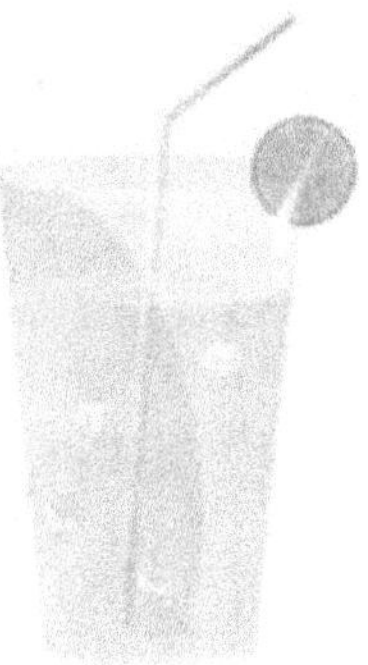

The lemonade is refreshing.

chocolat chaud

hot chocolate

I drink hot chocolate every day.

milk-shake

milkshake

The milkshake has whipped cream.

eau

water

The water is not cold.

thé

tea

The tea is hot.

lait

milk

Milk is white.

bière

beer

The beer is foamy.

un soda

soda

The soda is fizzy.

smoothie

smoothie

The smoothie is a watermelon flavor.

milk-shake

milkshake

The milkshake has whipped cream.

lait de coco

coconut milk

The coconut milk is yummy.

du jus d'orange

orange juice

The orange juice is made from oranges.

cacao

cocoa

The cocoa is sweet.

fromage

cheese

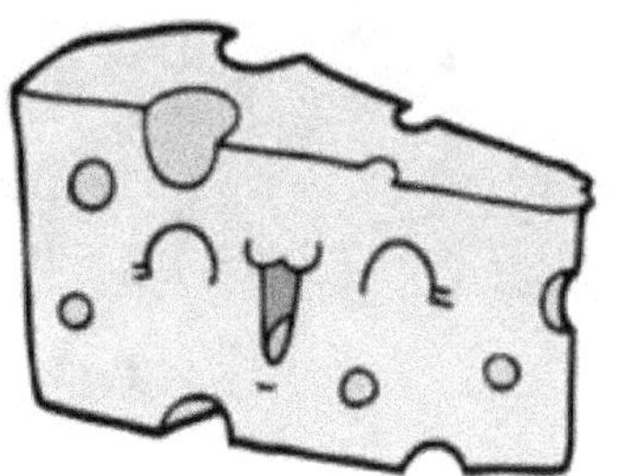

The cheese is creamy.

oeuf

egg

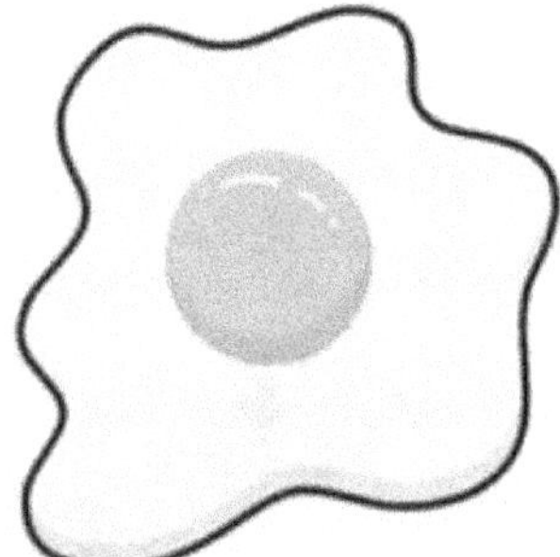

The egg is fried.

beurre

butter

The butter is put on bread.

margarine

margarine

Margarine looks like butter.

yaourt

yogurt

That yogurt is popular.

cottage cheese

cottage cheese

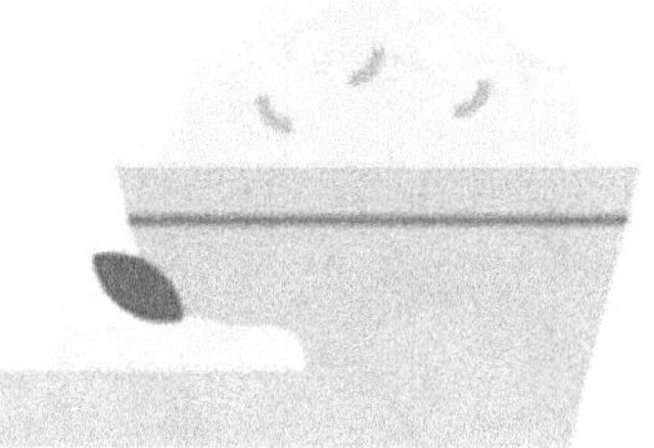

The cottage cheese is put on crackers.

crème glacée

ice cream

They have a triple scoop ice cream.

crème

cream

That is a lot of creams.

sandwich

sandwich

That sandwich is healthy.

saucisse

sausage

Americans love sausages.

hamburger

hamburger

That hamburger looks happy.

hot-dog

hot dog

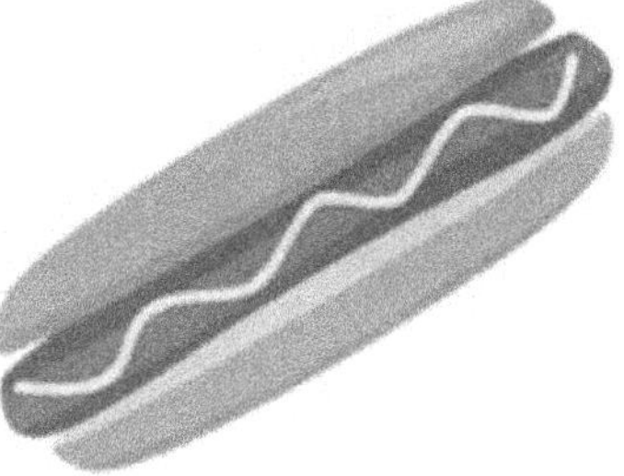

That hot dog has mustard on it.

pain

bread

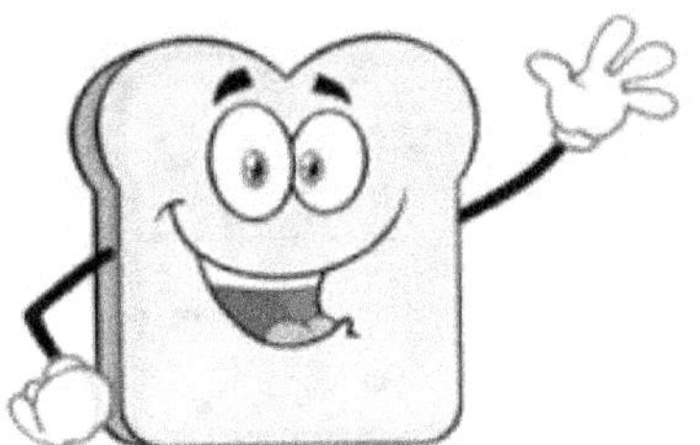

That bread is saying hello.

pizza

pizza

That pizza is cheesy.

steak

steak

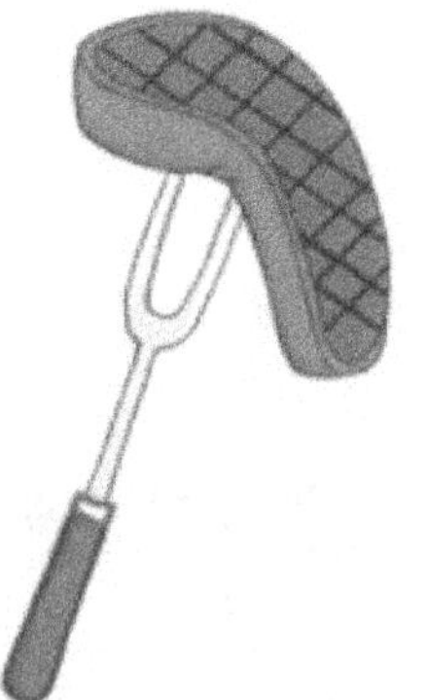

The steak was grilled.

poulet rôti

roast chicken

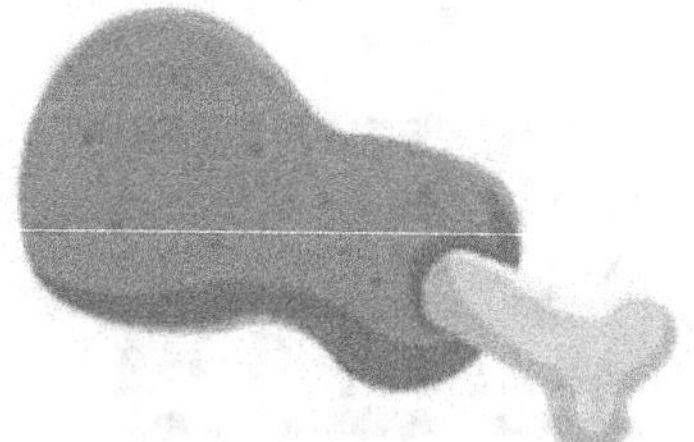

Roast Chicken is delicious.

poisson

fish

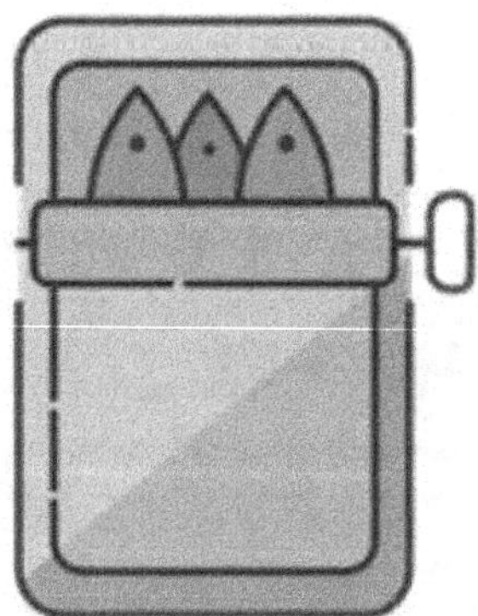

You can buy canned fish in the market.

fruit de mer

seafood

Lobster is expensive seafood.

jambon

ham

Ham can be put in sandwiches.

kebab

kebab

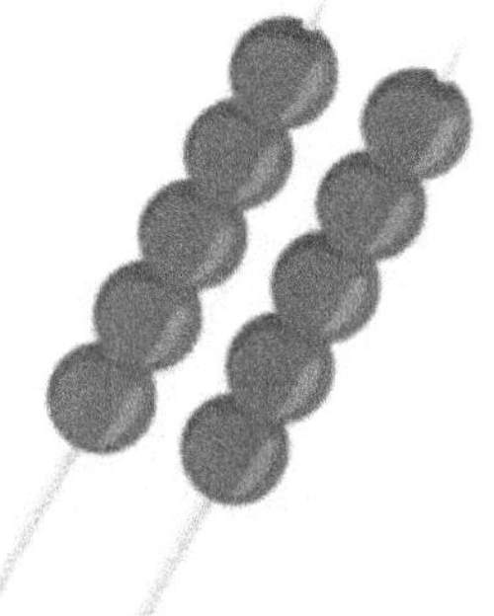

Kebab is a delicacy in America.

bacon

bacon

That bacon is smiling.

crème fraîche

sour cream

You can dip your chips in sour cream.

vache

cow

Cows are black and white.

lapin

rabbit

That rabbit is fun to play with.

canard

duck

That duck is content.

crevette

shrimp

The shrimp has six legs.

porc

pig

That pig is pink and fat.

abeille

bee

The bee has a stinger.

chèvre

goat

That goat has a white horn.

crabe

crab

The crab has two big pincers.

cerf

deer

That deer is sleeping.

dinde

turkey

The turkey has a giant tail.

colombe

dove

That dove is carrying a plant.

mouton

sheep

That sheep has fluffy wool.

poisson

fish

That fish has colorful fins.

That chicken is waking everybody up.

The horse has a red mane.

That wing chair is yellow.

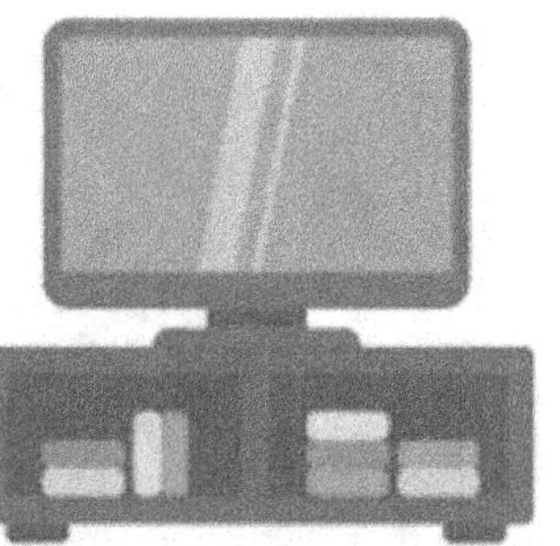

The TV stand can hold books.

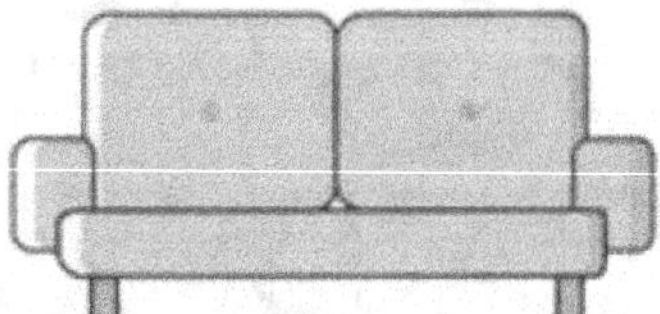

The sofa is comfortable to sit on.

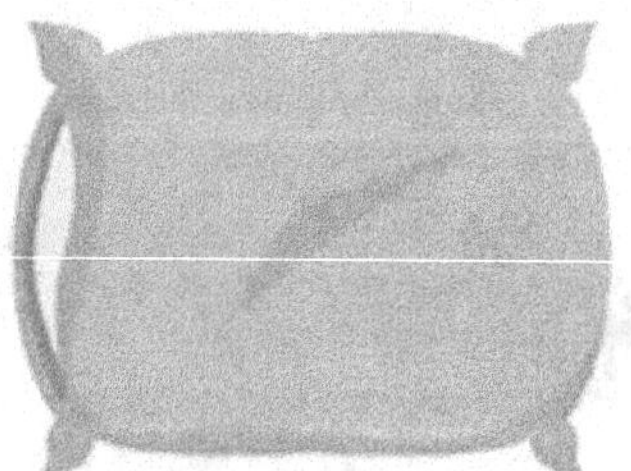

The cushion helps soften your seat.

téléphone

telephone

The telephone is ringing.

télévision

television

That television is big.

haut-parleurs

speaker

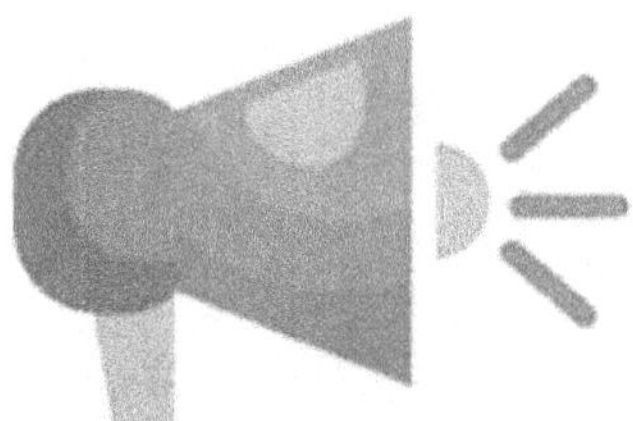

That speaker is used to increase the volume.

table d'appoint

end table

That end table is sparkling clean.

service à thé

tea set

That tea set is from China.

cheminée

fireplace

The fireplace makes me warm.

télécommandes

remote

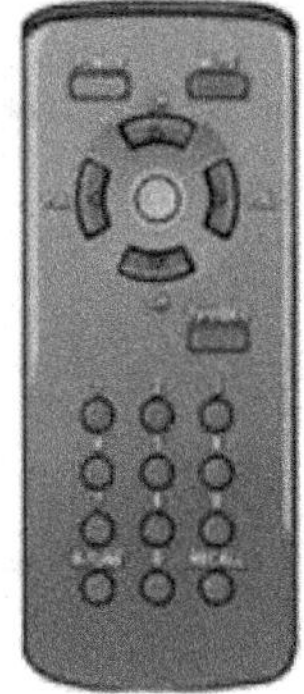

The remote has lots of buttons.

ventilateur électrique

fan

The fan is blowing wind.

lampadaire

floor lamp

The floor lamp is very tall.

tapis

carpet

The carpet is soft and silky.

bureaux

table

The table is made of wood.

stores

blinds

I will pull the blinds down.

rideaux

curtains

She opened the curtains.

image

picture

The picture is about the mountains and the sky.

vase

vase

The roses are all in a vase.

l'horloge

clock

The alarm clock is beeping.

oreiller

pillow

The pillow is pink and yellow.

cintre

hat stand

The hat stand has only one hat on it.

mettre la table

dressing table

I have made up on my dressing table.

lampe de table

table lamp

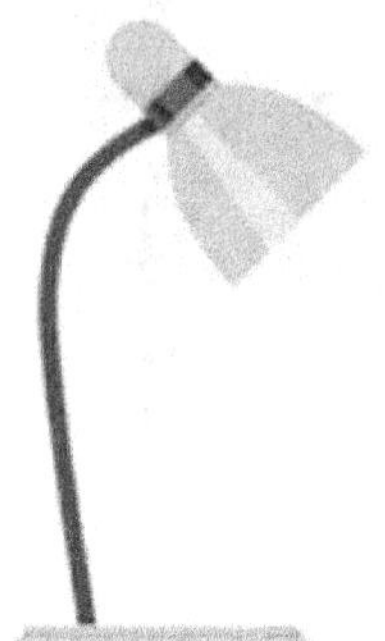

The table lamp will help me see in the dark.

miroir

mirror

The mirror is very tall.

planche a repasser

ironing board

Don't touch the ironing board, it's hot!

boîte avec tiroir

hope chest

You can keep your clothes in the hope chest.

table de chevet

night table

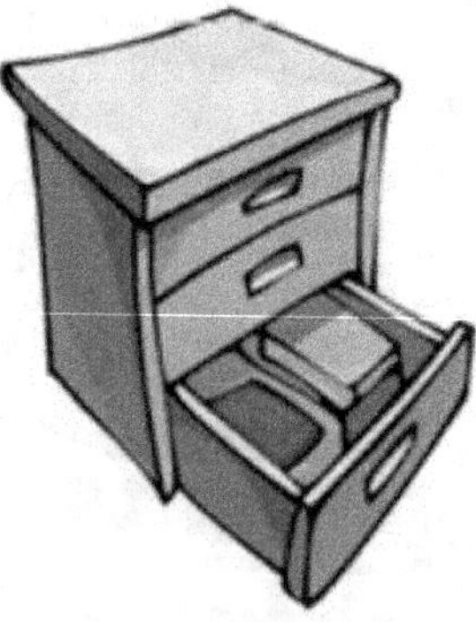

The nightstand has my lamp on it.

lit

bed

The bed is charming.

climatisation

air-conditioner

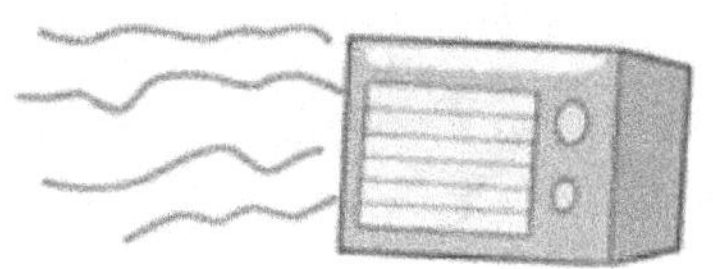

The air conditioner is cold.

cruche

jug

The measuring jug has nothing inside.

dentifrice

toothpaste

The toothpaste is mint flavored.

brosse à dents

toothbrush

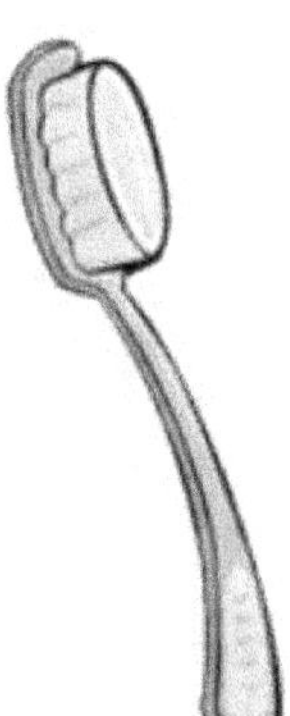

The toothbrush has toothpaste on it.

savon

soap

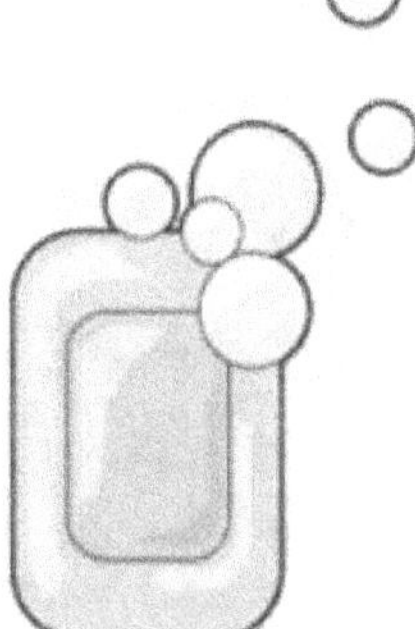

The soap is very bubbly.

pince à linge

clothespin

The clothespin will clip my clothes.

cintre

hanger

The hanger is hanging my boots.

sèche-cheveux

hair dryer

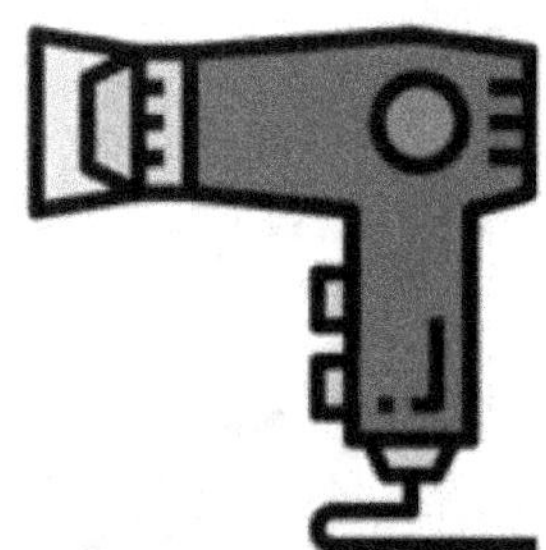

The hairdryer will blow my hair.

shampooing

shampoo

The shampoo is used to clean your hair.

bulle

bubble

The bubbles are very fun to play in.

brosse

brush

She is brushing her hair with the brush.

papier toilette

toilet paper

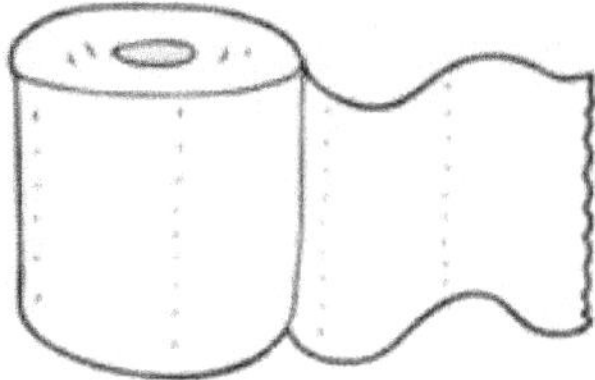

The toilet paper is used to dry your hands.

serviette

towel

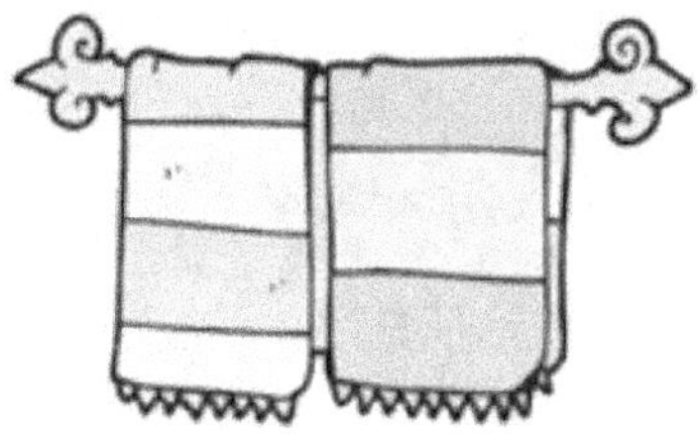

We have two towels on the rack.

corde à linge

clothesline

My shirt is hanging on the clothesline.

douche

shower

The shower is spraying water.

baignoire

bathtub

The bathtub is comfortable.

lessive

laundry detergent

The laundry detergent is used with the washing machine.

seau

bucket

Can you help me fill up the bucket?

vadrouilles

mops

The mop is used for mopping the floor.

savon liquide

liquid soap

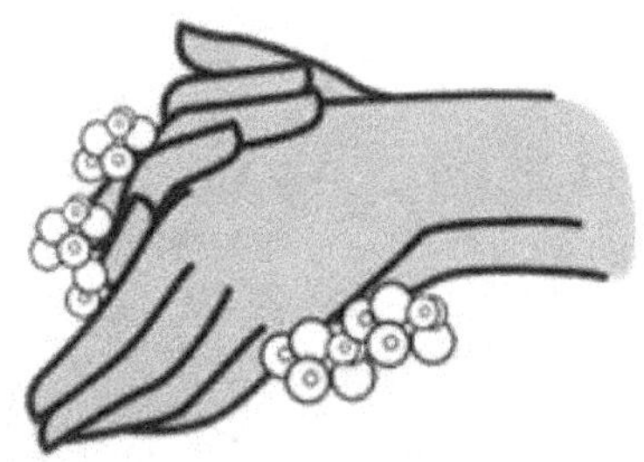

I use soapy water to wash my hands.

lessive en poudre

washing powder

I will scoop up the washing powder.

sac poubelle

trash bag

The trash bag is full of trash.

poubelle

trash can

You have only to put recylcle trash in the trash can.

les puits

sinks

You should wash your hands in the sink.

cuvette des toilettes

toilet bowl

She let her bunny use the toilet.

machine à laver

washing machine

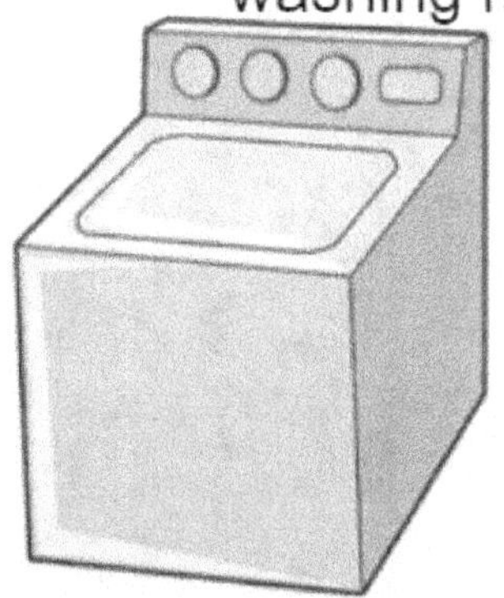

The washing machine wash your clothes.

panier à linge

laundry basket

She is putting all the clothes into the laundry basket.

le rasoir

razor

He uses the razor to shave his beard.

rasoir électrique

electric razor

The electric razor works faster than the normal one.

crème à raser

shaving cream

The shaving cream is fluffy.

bain de bouche

mouthwash

The mouthwash smells very lovely.

coton-tige

cotton bud

Q-tip can be used for many things.

brosse à cheveux

hair brush

She brushes her hair with her hairbrush.

peigne

comb

Her dad will comb her hair for her.

nettoyant

cleanser

Put the cap back on the cleanser bottle.

échelle

scale

You can measure things on the scale.

papier de soie

tissue paper

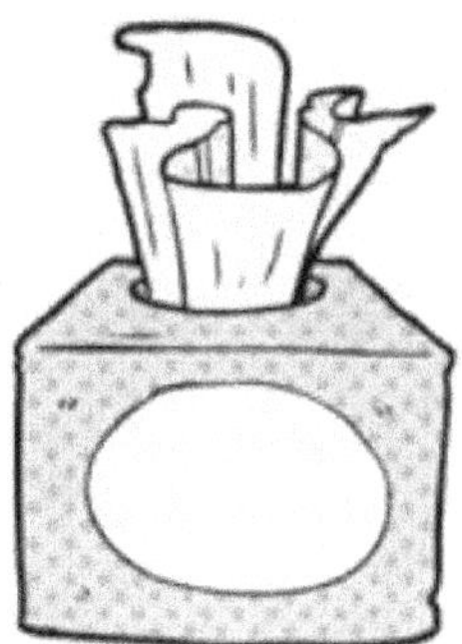

The tissue is on the counter.

jouets de bain

bath toys

The little duck is a bath toy.

robinet

faucet

The faucet is broken.

miroir

mirror

He is looking in the mirror.

tapis de bain

bath mat

The bath mat is purple and yellow.